Gutter feelings

Gutter feelings

Christian Youth Work in the Inner City

Pip Wilson

Marshalls

Marshalls Paperbacks
Marshall Morgan & Scott
3 Beggarwood Lane, Basingstoke, Hants, RG23 7LP, UK

ISBN 0 551 01282 X

Typeset by Brian Robinson, North Marston, Bucks
Printed in Great Britain by
Anchor Brendon Ltd, Tiptree, Essex

Contents

Preface

Lots of young people feel what I call 'gutter feelings', and so do I. This book traces my life from my own youth, my Christian conversion and its influence throughout my youth work especially. It isn't a success story! It is not even a story – more of a reflection of what I have learned from personal experience, the people around me and Jesus Himself.

It is written to reach non-academic readers, as well as theological and youth work students and practitioners. I pick up real life issues and try not to dodge them. The names of most of our young people have been changed.

I want to acknowledge my appreciation to the past and present members of the teams at 'Y' club, St Helens YMCA and Mayflower. They have given and shared their lives with me to make all the beautiful experiences possible.

I want to say the biggest 'Fanx' to Annabel Jackson, Joy Sansom and Liz Ward who have typed the manuscript, besides giving the advice that it needed at least one full stop! Without their encouragement and practical help it wouldn't have been completed at all.

To Joan, Joy and Ann who are the closest loving family that anyone can have – I dedicate this to them.

Pip Wilson
April 1985

Foreword

Pip Wilson, through this book, aims to reach non-academic readers as well as others; to face real life and to reflect on his last ten years as Senior Youth Leader at the Mayflower in London's East End. His fourth declared aim is to appreciate others. All these aims are unquestionably achieved.

For us both, having lived and worked on the same patch of ground in the 50s and 60s for twelve years, the opportunity to hear and feel the experience of another since we left was not one to be missed. To have been asked to write a joint Foreword says a great deal about Pip's view of partnership in this context. It is a view that we share, and having read the book, feel honoured to have been approached.

Pip's statement, 'I am a realistic Christian with "hope", not an optimist', is telling. It is possible to be both a pessimist and also full of hope. The book not only justifies but explains what this means. A number of Christians are heard to say despairingly, 'But what can we do?' One of Pip's answers is, 'Please try to understand and listen while we tell you what it is like, how it is.' Being a youth leader is more than ever today very lonely and costly work and it needs systematic and regular support.

For a youth leader to share himself with the people he loves, young East Londoners, so completely, and also to share that experience with many of us over the years in regular newsletters is in itself a considerable achievement in communication and in energy. And now the reflections are drawn together in *Gutter Feelings* in a way which makes the book hard to put down. It is clear that Pip has carried a great deal personally. He has skilfully woven together the importance of being on 'the underside' of interdependence of family and colleagues, and of Jesus Christ.

But the sad reflection is that, apart from the local church members, the Church as an institution does not seem to have demonstrated its support or understanding of the scale of difficulties and blocks which whole communities face. These difficulties he rightly indicates are injustices. Great store is being set on the Archbishop's Commission on *Urban Priority Areas Report*, due to be published in December. It appears to be an object of real hope to the Pip Wilsons of this world. The Church is putting its weight into listening and understanding: it is reaching out in a world that has long since felt alienated and judged. Church members will be given a unique opportunity to share in the listening and to respond. *Gutter Feelings* is a natural and refreshingly open way-in to the *Report*. It is not general but deeply rooted in real people's lives: people who live and breathe on 'the underside' of our society.

Youth leaders, judges, criminals, bishops, pensioners and politicians, and anyone considering marriage to a youth leader or clergyman, all will find this book easy to read and a place in it for them. It is about the possibility of the Kingdom of God on earth. There is an invitation to stay and listen and share the feelings that are uncompromisingly and lovingly offered. There is an authenticity to the text borne out by the recording of actual events and experiences while they were fresh in Pip's mind.

Being subject to relentless prejudice and disregard makes people hard on the outside and inevitably produces emotional handicap. The expression of this handicap is undoubtedly violence. This book helps towards understanding what makes people violent and some ways of coping with it. Pip's plea to share his feelings of hurt when some people label other people as hooligans, louts and yobbos is clear. It is a profoundly Christian viewpoint and has nothing to do with 'do-gooders' being soft. The reader will find very little softness experienced by the night and day commitment of youth workers like Pip and Joan and their colleagues. It is a much softer option, and infinitely more patronising to dismiss those who show such love as do-gooders.

If we believe that Jesus came to earth to meet people, to live and feel with them, to share His life and not dodge the pain; if we believe that He came to listen and to understand with the limited and human life-span that we have; if we believe that He used the spiritual resources available to all of us, then we cannot fail to feel closer to the people whose lives are shared with us in this book. The words 'Thy Kingdom come' that we say so often take on new meaning. They become active and stir us to work as well as to wait for the Kingdom. God's Kingdom on earth is about there being a place for everyone. *Gutter Feelings* expresses a problem in graphic terms. The problem is that to so many people the Kingdom of God is not for anyone who is violent, badly behaved or law-breaking. Unless other people reach out with their lives and commitment and love as Pip has done, then whole communities will grow up believing God to be a policeman, a judge or a government who wants only to imprison them. As Pip says, 'If we are not part of the solution, we are part of the problem.'

This is not a success story. It is a love story: a modern day Gospel story with roots. There is a challenge to all of us in the Church to join forces more tangibly by exercising this kind of love with our prayer, our money, ourselves and our power. Youth workers need systematic support. They have to have courage.

If as a Church we disregard the people on 'the underside' who have so much to give us, we do so at our peril.

David and Grace Sheppard
Liverpool
July 1985.

1: Youth to youth worker

It was an ordinary evening at the club, but it was obvious that trouble was brewing. I turned round from chatting to a group of kids to see what seemed to be a mass of bodies involved in something that looked horrible. Someone was picking up pool balls and hurling them violently towards a boy who was already being kicked and punched by four or five others.

A fight had started in the club and I had known it was coming. The atmosphere had been tense all evening. Included among the 200 teenagers present we had a large group of older teenage boys who were out to prove themselves. They stood in a large group in a dominant area overlooking the disco and social area. Their only form of communication was foul language and a kick for anyone who was passing. There was bound to be trouble sooner or later.

You can't just 'police' in a hostile environment like this. Your emotions are stretched, you try to keep your eyes everywhere and yet you need to *seem* relaxed and active. This was my position when the fight broke out. An Asian-looking boy had come into the club with two white girls. Asians normally never enter the Mayflower club, but due to the extensive publicity with the smart new club opening, one or two had started coming and we had been pleased to welcome them. Normally they didn't stay long because of the racist abuse and harassment that we were unable to control.

Alan, Doug and Geoff (my full-time colleagues) and myself were into the mêlée instantly and it stopped briefly before more violent kicks and punches were thrown at the badly bleeding and shaken visitor. He was taken down to my office by Doug while the other workers tried to deal with the violent and bitter racist atmosphere. 'We were only pulling others off him,' said the four regular club members, grinning sickly. We had got to know these boys over the previous five years, loved them, prayed for them and yet they were still violent, aggressive teenagers.

In the office I tried desperately to relate to a young man who was highly agitated, insulted, bitter, humiliated and covered in blood. Doug was bandaging him, for he was bleeding badly from a head wound caused by a pool ball. I tried to apologise, explain, express our hurt, before he was driven away to hospital in a quickly borrowed minibus. The bitter racist atmosphere was still evident in the club. There were laughs from both sexes. 'Did you see him bleed? His blood was black!' 'The next best thing to a dead dog is a dead Paki!' It is impossible to express the immensity of hurt and hate evident that evening.

During his journey to the hospital Doug found out that the young man's nationality was South American! It didn't matter to the attackers—he *looked* like a Paki! The club continued but we knew quite well that we would have to stand with this young visitor against our members. Justice meant our standing against any racist attack and this justice was instantly offered to the visitor.

The next day was even worse. There were two probation officers in my office when the four boys concerned with the attack came round, having heard that the police were after them, and realising our obvious involvement as witnesses.

Threats were directed at me with such ferocity that it shook me to the core. Inside I was shaking. I am certain that if the probation officers hadn't been there the attack would have been physical, and I felt protected by their presence. 'We are coming to smash the place up Sunday,' were their parting words.

All this resulted in some horrible days. The members concerned were known to be going through a very violent time of their lives. It affected me deeply. I was unable to sleep for two nights; I was afraid to walk the streets; I was scared for our kids. Joan, my wife, was waking up in the middle of the night and retching in the toilet. The tension for my family was so great – yet it was second-hand tension, all being passed on from me.

The police were involved, not only in searching for the attackers, but we also had to bring plain clothes police into the club for protection. In the East End culture you can do no worse than 'grass' on someone. That was what we were seen to be doing – and for a 'Paki' too. But we believed in justice – God's justice.

The tension lasted some weeks because after arrest the boys were released on bail pending their trial, which would be months later.

Later the same week I was in the disco crowded with lots of young teenagers enjoying themselves when Joan, one of our youth workers, pushed through to me. 'Pip, Jon is in and he's got a knife . . .' She took the office key to phone the 'Old Bill' (police) and I sat on the window ledge in the disco, hiding in our own club as teenagers danced around me. Five years of work with teenagers in East London and I needed to hide out of the way. I felt sick. At the same time, one of my experienced, professionally-trained colleagues was also hiding, sitting on the floor of the office, shaking. All of us were emotionally stunned and yet we would have to face another day, the same teenagers and other teenagers, because we all live in the same community.

This is just one incident in my life and there will be many more as you read on. However, I've tried not just to relate incidents, but also my struggle to understand, as a Christian and a youth worker, why they happen and to form some positive response to them.

I've worked with young people full-time now for twenty years – usually with kids who are seen as 'delinquent' or 'tough'. The hard, tough image outside is a big front, it seems to me – inside there is a sensitive delicate human being who is hurting.

In my childhood I hurt too. Having three older brothers I felt 'underside', that is, quite insignificant. I had to be aggressive at school and in the street because I knew no other response other than to be a nobody, a 'wimp' in today's language, or as we used to say in St Helens, 'mard', which roughly translates as soft, or cissy.

I came from a warm accepting home, with a mum who taught warmth by example. My dad was a coal mine worker, who worked hard to keep our family. He wore a leather belt around his waist, and he occasionally used it on his children!

I didn't do well at school. At the age of ten or eleven I still couldn't read, so my mum paid Albert, a local grammar school boy, half a crown to give me a Saturday morning lesson. We used to sneak in and listen to 'Dick Barton Special Agent' on the wireless. He was the dashing, super-hero of those days! Dick Barton didn't get me through my 11-plus exam though! Learning didn't come easy – but I did eventually learn to read and I was grateful for that.

Like most working class youngsters I picked up 'street skills' as I grew up, but I also had an outlet with my rugby.

I played at school and also for the best Rugby League team in the world! Blackbrook Amateur Rugby Club which beat every team in our age group and cultivated some of the best professional Rugby League players, who remain famous in the sport.

Being a clever rugby player wasn't my game however. I was a prop forward, or second row forward, but most renowned as a hooker – a dirty one! It was a big macho sport and I was given credibility for my tackling, fighting and getting sent off. I boasted of butting a Lancashire County scrum half so hard that he never played again. I boasted of hitting my opposing prop so hard, in every scrum, that I could get the loose head – or control of the scrum without the usual skilful play. Smashing mud into a hooker's eyes and mouth during the scrum was my speciality. Even now, as I write, I am aware that I can, if I don't watch it, actually enjoy relating all this – rather than having an awareness of succumbing to my own macho stereotyping.

But I had to be good at something. If I had been brought up in the East End of London I guess I would have been good at street fighting and thieving, the local street skills, rather than the cultural violence of St Helens. My violence was not obvious law breaking. It was contained within an aggressive sport.

John McVicar is a year younger than me and was born in the East End of London. He was best known as 'The Most Wanted Man in Britain' and 'Public Enemy Number One'. He made a spectacular escape from the maximum security prison at Durham and, on his recapture, was sentenced to a total of twenty-six years.

Having taken a Sociology degree, McVicar has become equipped to evaluate his own childhood[1] and I have learned much from him. Like him, I threw myself into sport and a macho lifestyle, although he differed from me in that he

13

became more anti-authority at school. His education was also far superior to mine and to that of most of the East End young people that I know today.

During these exciting adolescent years I had kept contact with my local Boys' Brigade (B.B.) company run by a local man, Clive Rimmer. He didn't just welcome the 'nice' kids – he had street kids as well, the ones who liked sport and a good game of mat rugby in the church hall (mat rugby involved two teams, two mats, one ball and no rules!). Even during the days of little or no attendance at B.B. during my excursions to Butlins Holiday Camps, rugby training and games, I remained acceptable and accepted at B.B. That was flexibility of leadership in action! So often working-class kids are 'kicked out' of Christian organisations because they don't have the commitment, consistency or regularity! Clive was the one who put so much spadework in on me and my mates, although I guess without much joy or apparent 'success'.

One night at B.B. I was pulled into the kitchen/office in the church hall. The vicar, Rev Frank Llewellyn Jones, was there, and Clive, the Captain.

'Pip, we've had so much disruption and trouble from you – we've got to kick you out . . . or . . . or promote you to some position of responsibility in the organisation! Other NCOs in the B.B. tell us that you wouldn't accept a promotion to Lance Corporal – so we are offering you a promotion to full Corporal.'

That was the beginning of leadership for me. I was introduced to leadership, within structures, with support but nevertheless I was responsible for and to a group of young boys. And I was only fifteen myself!

During my time as a Boys' Brigade N.C.O., Warrant Officer and Officer, it seems to me now that I was being trained – experiential training mainly. I learned the basics of small group leadership: speaking, handling a large group, organisation and the benefit of monthly team meetings, which I have continued ever since. Most of my leadership was intuitive because I was indigenous to that culture. But I will always be grateful for that early opportunity for leadership for, to quote from one of our local young people; 'Ain't it true that if you treat people responsibly they do things responsible?'

In 1960 I was still a B.B. Officer, now aged twenty-one, single, still playing rugby, boozing a lot and enjoying life. For some reason I didn't go to Butlins Holiday Camp that year – so I went to North Wales on the B.B. camp week.

My mate Pee was an Officer too and we shared a tent. He's a funny fella, he reminds me of a roll of film – undeveloped!! [He even thinks that ducks don't fly upside down because they would quack up!!] Something happened to us both that week. The camp chaplain, Norman Meeten, was a young curate – and I respected him immediately. He was an ex-Royal Marine Commando and that fitted my macho stereotyping. He was tough and agile; he could walk over mountains as if he'd been born there. Yet he was quiet! And he had presence!

One evening the officers were standing around in the marquee while the hundred boys were settling down in bed. I was chatting in one group but started to listen to conversations in a nearby group. Norman was talking and I could hear him saying that God was a real person, so real that he could affect our daily lives. He was giving examples of this – how God had actually provided money, on time and the right amount! I think at that moment I became aware of an alive God. Previous to that, people I knew were either churchgoers or not, religious or not. But I kept those thoughts to myself. I don't remember much more, other than that the next day or so I sat in a group of people and heard Norman talk about John Chapter Three in the Bible and for the first time I heard that we needed to be 'born again'. It seemed very important because Jesus said it must be so – not just Norman Meeten. It said that it wasn't sufficient to be born once as a child; we needed an additional rebirth later in life.

That week Pee, my best mate, walked into the tent and said he'd become a Christian. It hit me right between the eyes. It could happen to ordinary people! That must have brought it really close. If it could happen to Pee it could happen . . . to me.

It didn't just then. I left B.B. camp quite stunned – but thinking. Then two weeks later I knelt late one night by the side of my bed and talked personally to God and asked him to do something, because I knew I was missing out on something good.

The next day I was walking around expecting to feel and be different. Other than a feeling of anticlimax nothing had changed! I think the next significant thing was when someone said to me, 'If you believe in God, now you need to believe He has done something, and trust Him a bit.'

This may be a bit strange to non-Christian readers. Let me explain. The Bible tells us that when we become Christians, Jesus actually comes and lives inside our bodies. Romans 8:9 puts it well – I love the Living Bible version: 'Anyone who hasn't got the Spirit of Christ in him, is not a Christian at all'. That means if He lives in there – you are a Christian (Christ-in = Christian!). There is something incredible about this. I've never got over it! The Bible even says why He chooses to enter into ordinary people: 'Yet we who have this spiritual treasure are like common clay pots, in order to show that the supreme power belongs to God, not to us.' (2 Cor. 4:7). He, the Maker, chooses to live inside ordinary people like me (and you!).

There is no doubt about it in my mind, this experience has been my major motivator for the rest of my life. I've had to change in many phases over the years, but Jesus has always been central and alive. It's different for different people, because we are all unique individuals, but that's how it happened to me in 1960.

In youth work I often tell the story of the young man who had an old Ford car that often let him down. One day, as he sat by the roadside unable to get it going, an old man pulled up in a brand new Ford car and offered to help. 'This rotten car always lets me down,' the young chap said to the distinguished older man. The man looked inside the bonnet, fiddled for a bit, asked for a screwdriver and then asked for ignition. The young man was so pleased to hear the engine start. 'Thanks so much for all your help. My name is George Williams and I'm really grateful to you.' 'I'm only too pleased to be of assistance,' the old man said. 'My name is Henry Ford.'

Henry Ford was the maker, creator and designer of the Ford car and so he knew how to put it right. *Our* Creator can put *us* right! That's the message and since 1960 that's been fact for me. He is still repairing me and making me whole.

From then on I wasn't just a voluntary youth worker – I was an alive, motivated, purposeful youth worker.

I still worked at 'The Vulcan', a large engineering factory near St Helens, where I had a good rugby playing mate whom we called 'Belch' because his surname was Belcher. After my camp week, on my first day back at work Belch leaned over his big turret lathe and shouted over the noise as I worked on mine. He was asking why I had stopped using the usual swear words. I hadn't really noticed myself, but I'd just naturally stopped using the normal factory vocabulary and Belch had noticed. When I told him the reason he got all our mates and lining up they walked in slow procession, with hands together in mock piety, around my machine.

That didn't bother me, for it wasn't a concept I'd got hold of – it was something concrete: a relationship that was real, not just a nice thought. I wasn't interested in repentance, redemption, etc. They are words I still don't bother about. I had fallen in love with a person – Jesus, and that was a real concrete experience.

By the age of twenty-two I had started 'kissing'. Joan Williams was this girl who lived up the same street and always seemed to have plenty of boyfriends, including my mate Pee! I was the comedian of the gang and not particularly good at 'pulling birds', to use a phrase that reflects my typical sexist attitude at that time.

But then Joan and I, helped by a mutual friend's introduction, started going out together – driving to our first date at the famous Cavern Club in Liverpool. In those days the Beatle-type groups were support bands to 'trad' Jazz bands. Yes, it was a case of 'She loves you – yeah, yeah, yeah!', even though it took us a year or so cautiously to declare our love for each other.

Joan had quite a rough time courting this arrogant, extrovert, rugby playing, boozing (and yet Christian) boyfriend. I was so proud, hard and emotionally tough. Sometimes after a rugby match I would turn up hours late for a date, often the worse the wear for drink. My relationship with God was similarly alcohol-affected. I used to pray and read a bit of the Bible every night, but often swaying on my knees due to Greenall's bitter!

I can look back now and wonder at God's incredible

acceptance of me as I was. I never felt rejected by my Lord – I felt He just encouraged me, with no put-downs. Joan too, although sometimes upset and devalued by me, accepted me as I was while steadily working on my growth and maturity. We were courting for three years before we were married at our local church. 'To God be the glory, great things He has done,' we sang.

We had mortgaged a terraced house 500 yards from the church – going against the social norm of moving out to the more suburban areas. Our life then was centred on playing a God-guided rôle in our local church, including leading Bible studies in undecorated rooms, with paint cans for seats. The Rolling Stones were new in those days and many late nights were spent hearing inferior versions from teenagers standing in front of the lounge mirror. Joan was involved in Junior B.B. and worked at Pilkington's head office. I was now Captain of the B.B. and working in a good job for Pilkington Glass in their research laboratories. Clive, my first B.B. leader, had entered theological college to train in the Anglican ministry.

Chapter 1

References

1. John McVicar, *McVicar by Himself* (Arrow 1974/79).

2: At work

'The Rocking Vicar' they used to call me at work – always singing the latest pop songs above the machine noise, and yet strangely religious! I always enjoyed work, both the challenge of my trade and the stimulus of factory discussion. And I never felt uncomfortable about talking about Jesus. He was and is an everyday person.

Joan and I did always feel, however, that evening and weekend work with kids was always more fulfilling than the jobs we both had at Pilkington Glass.

On our honeymoon we bought the *Daily Mail*, which was unusual as my Dad (who died when I was seventeen) always read the *Daily Mirror* and both parents now read the *Daily Express*. We saw in it an advert for a job in an Approved School in Cheshire. We discussed it, but agreed that it was not for us. Strangely, however, during the following months, as the school in Cheshire developed, we continued to see adverts for staff and became more aware of the school. It seemed that God was directing us towards these adverts and although we had no qualifications we decided to apply for a job 'in faith'. The day we got the job as houseparents at Mobberley Boys' School we were stupefied, numbed! One year to the day of moving into our first home, we moved out to live in an institution belonging to Manchester Children's Department, now part of Social Services.

Joan was twenty-two and I was twenty-six. She was

housemother to between fifteen and thirty boys, and her work included cooking for them. I was housefather and responsible for the same boys during all out of school hours.

It was a fascinating period of our lives. God provided another Christian couple on the staff – Ann and Paul Delight. He was chaplain and housefather in a nearby block. It is good how God doesn't plan for us to be alone.

It was a large school of 120 boys between thirteen and seventeen. We had thirty boys in four houses with three sets of houseparents to a house. We learned so much at Mobberley from fellow staff. How to run an institution, how not to sit or stand with your back to the boys, how to pray with your eyes open, how to oppress kids into a routine for the comfort of the staff. I learned how to search a bedroom to find contraband cigarettes in the hollow chairlegs or wardrobe coatrail. I learned how to 'read' young people's behaviour and to be constantly alert in their presence. Unfortunately I also had to experience the humiliation of young boys removing their underpants so that they could be caned six times with only the regulation shorts as protection.

We met really deprived inner city kids for the first time – every one of them different! The blue-eyed, red-cheeked, blond-haired angel face who had arson tendencies and convictions. The square-jawed, steel-eyed, unruly-haired quiet type with manslaughter convictions. Also the black kid! Never before had I been in contact with a black person. Incredibly, at twenty-six years old I had never met a black person! I can picture many kids now as I write. They were different from most St Helens kids I had met – much harder emotionally. Not necessarily harder fighters, but deeper, more severe – on the surface alive but underneath dying. It seemed to me that I was meeting real emotional handicap for the first time.

When you give, you learn. The approved school days were full of giving and learning. We enjoyed the challenge of life there. Also we were delighted to see several of the boys place their lives in God's grip.

Paul, for instance, was a black, illegitimate, energetic boy. He never walked through a door – he came through it as if he lived to destroy door hinges! His normal bright eyes used often to spark with defiance and confrontation was inevitable. Paul was 'underside', (inadequate, at the bottom), came from a rough part of Manchester and a one parent family. He loved his mum. I can see him now waiting for her to arrive. Nervous, bouncing up and down with apprehension and dressed up in his school best, only to be let down again when she didn't arrive. We shared his hurt and loneliness in that institution. There was little we could say. *She* was his mum. We were the authorities – symbols of oppression. Once Paul's mum came unexpectedly to school on his birthday loaded with a large crate of food. In his sullen anger he refused to touch it. He had been rejected so often he had hardened himself against further hurt.

It was good to see Paul become a Christian in that environment. His life became meaningful, although he got some 'stick' from his mates. One of his problems was finding time for reading his Bible, which he was keen to do. At bedtime there was a strict routine and early morning was even worse. The boys had to stay in bed until the lights went on and then line up in the corridor for the count, then go down to the washroom for their strip wash. Then there was the ritual of dress, bed-making, bed-checking, breakfast, house cleaning and then to school for the day. I found out that before the lights went on in the morning, Paul was tucking his Bible down his pyjamas and going down to sit on the toilet where he could read with the light on!

As with most conversions among working-class young people, Paul was up and down with his faith. He'd throw God back at me when we had a row and yet a few hours later his smile and the twinkle in his eye told me that he hadn't given up on me or his God. In his erratic life it was important for both me and his Lord to be consistent.

We kept contact with Paul for some years after he left the school. We even went to visit him and his wife in Manchester and there were return visits to us.

I loved those boys, but I confess that at times I used to lose my temper and belt some of them across the face. It was one way, in my limited repertoire, of dealing with confrontation. It was a different situation to the one I was to experience in youth work in East London. In the approved school I was 'in charge' and there to impose authority upon young people who had no choice as to their attendance. In Canning Town the young people chose to come to the club and as a youth worker I didn't see my rôle as an imposer of authority, but one of a social educator trying to develop self-control.

In the early years at Mayflower I have physically confronted, and fought, the biggest and toughest teenagers who are now violent, professional criminals. In later years we developed a team principle of not physically ejecting any kids from the club. So what do you do when someone sprays ammonia, takes drugs, spits in someone's face and starts a whole package of trouble? That isn't a hypothetical question when doing youth work in East London.

The point is that no matter what the physical size of the person we deal with, no matter what status we possess, our response to them needs to be one of love, not oppression. It's so easy to be in control when dealing with small children, the aged and perhaps the physically and mentally handicapped. The very violent and aggressive youths I have met have challenged all my methods and attitudes. Feeling powerless and not 'in control' has affected my whole life and love principle. Jesus' Kingdom is a Kingdom of love, not one where power rules and people compete.

So often leaders are in a position of power and authority. Have you experienced leadership when *you* are not able to compete? Where you feel totally inadequate? This is the feeling of being 'underside'.

Chris Sugden of The Oxford Centre for Mission Studies spoke at a Frontier Youth Trust National Event in 1983 and said that Christians need to read the Bible from the *underside* instead of reading it from a position of power, or *topside*: i.e. from the viewpoint of the middle class, waged, sheltered, well-fed and comfortable.

Joan and I loved those kids in the approved school, prayed for them, gave them all we had in time and space. And yet the wholeness that they required of us we didn't possess for ourselves. Being Christians wasn't enough. God used us right there and on time – but He has much more to give to us, the disciples. Part of that 'wholeness road' was the pain of the underside that was yet to come. At the approved school I was in power. Junior staff, but in power and topside.

Andrew Kirk said at Greenbelt Arts Festival, 1984, that, 'people who are employed, comfortable, have money and status – they pray for *peace*. People who are unemployed, uncomfortable, no money or status – they pray for *justice*!' Depending on where we stand in society, there is a difference in how we read the Bible, pray, talk and act.

Jim Wallis says 'the truth about society is best known at the bottom'[1]. Often in frontier youth work you feel at the bottom. So often being with kids every day who are desperately bored, devalued in unemployment, living only for drugs, it gets into your system. You begin to weep with those who weep. When you get physically attacked and feel powerless in the hands of the street kids, who in themselves are on the bottom rung of society, you feel yourself at the bottom – the underside.

When we are in this situation, that is when we read the Bible from the underside and identify with God who became flesh and dwelt among us and who also became the suffering servant.

'That sadness was used by God . . . For the sadness that is used by God brings a change of heart that leads to *salvation*' (2 Cor. 7:9, 10).

Joy, our eldest daughter, was born at Mobberley and the boys helped to bring her up. The crazy menu there, including pilchards for breakfast gave her flexible taste-buds! The kids loved Joy and enjoyed watching her growing up. Joan and I were delighted that it was them, the boys as a group, who encouraged her first ever step. She was aged one when we left Mobberley to return to St Helens for my first full-time youth work job. This was a much prayed-over decision to be confirmed later in the lives of young people.

We had seen this advertisement for a youth worker in our own home district with a flat on the job. It was a 'kneel down and pray' situation and we did that as we discovered God's will for us.

I was twenty-eight when we arrived at the YWCA Community Centre – the 'Y Club'. Five years of your life isn't easy to write about. We had taken the 'underside road' again. From two salaries down to one, at 'unqualified' rate. Another flat on the job, which meant always being available and constantly present on or off duty!

Pressure was all around us. We attracted lots of street teenagers – with all their luggage! One day in the flat I remember being so tense that I pulled down a picture from the wall and smashed it to pieces. I'd never done anything like that before – nor since. I was experiencing feelings of stress that I was untrained to cope with. I had little support, and the church didn't seem to understand the point of the work. Why not run church activities? Why run another building down the road? Why should church people be doing things out there? Frontier Youth Trust gave me considerable support during those days, and a theology that was relevant. Relevant to the sort of situations and kids that I was to be dealing with.

It was one Sunday night and we had our special evening in progress. The club wasn't normal on Sundays; we had a big education/film/discussion/preaching or similar session. The snooker and juke box came later. In the middle of all this walked a gang of rockers. They had been thrown out of Derbyshire Hill Youth Club, the Horseshoe pub and so on until they finally arrived at the 'Y' Club at the bottom of the road.

I was instantly attracted to them. Smiling faces, quick wit, their aggressive energy shone through their leather jacket and long-haired image. From then on the club grew into a 'rocker' venue. A small group of rocker boys started attending regularly and their girls came along too eventually. Long leather jackets and tight jeans was the fashion. It was a hard ground that needed a lot of ploughing. Seeds were sown, many being taken by the powers in the air, but others took root and grew tenfold. Willy Holland, one of the original group, is the present full-time worker and he and his wife Linda (ex-rockergirl) both do incredible Christian frontier youth work as indigenous leaders. Geoff Simms, another of that original group, is now a committed Christian and helps at the club.

Of course the great majority of them didn't become Christians. What of their lives now? I will probably never know. But I believe they saw and felt the Kingdom being lived out in that little back street club on an unmade road. That place that was open when the pubs closed, where you could chat till two or three in the morning. That place open Saturday and Sunday. That place where your vomit would be mopped up by Ron or Pip, and you might get a lift home in their car as well.

I remember one night when three of the girls hesitantly approached us. We had shown a sex education film the night before and they said, 'We're like it said on the film.' They meant that they were promiscuous, but they couldn't say it. Joan and I chatted to them and discovered that they were involved in 'gang bangs'. The gang they belonged to were using them sexually. So I talked it through with the boys and Joan with the girls until there was an acceptable change in behaviour.

All this was about establishing the Kingdom. All done in Jesus' name together with an authentic presence and proclamation of His concern for 'new life'. 'Seek first the Kingdom of God and His justice' was worked out at the 'Y' Club through incidents such as this 'gang bang' situation. And the 'heavenly Kingdom' came on the agenda all too often when yet another rocker died on his motorbike and we all went to the funeral. The Kingdom is the message, but also the method, the way to work it out.

It's sad to see Christians so knotted up about living their life to get to heaven. The Kingdom of Heaven is assured to us, it is the Kingdom upon earth that we need to work at. Some people see the Kingdom purely as something you get when you die. The Good News of the Kingdom that Jesus was talking about was not just His words but His whole life. Jesus didn't come just to die on the cross – but to live, and show it!

It was at the 'Y' Club that I renewed my contact with the

courts as I stood by the kids when they were in trouble. I had gained some experience of this in my approved school days. To stand alongside a seemingly confident, brash, tough teenager when he is vulnerable is a stand for justice.

William Temple (1967) said that 'the church is the only co-operative society that exists for the benefit of non-members'. It was so at the 'Y' Club. God's Good News of the Kingdom belonged to them, but they just didn't know it at the time.

After five years at the 'Y' Club we were feeling a bit battered. Lots to give (and to learn) but we knew it was time to go. Joan was pregnant with Ann and Joy was six.

I remember in those days that we prayed a lot for guidance about our future. One night in particular – it was bath time. Tom and Jerry TV time before going downstairs to let the rockers in! Joy and I had a routine. Bath first and then watch Tom and Jerry. I did my usual with Joy – stand her up in the bath and lather her from head to foot and then leave her to rinse and play until 'It's Tom and Jerry,' and in would come Joy, wrapped glamorously in her bathtowel.

This evening Joan and I prayed while Joy bathed. We just asked for the Lord's direction to become clear. We never did see Tom and Jerry that evening. A knock on the door interrupted our viewing. It was Denis Carnaby, who was General Secretary at St Helens YMCA, asking us if we would consider working with him at the YM.

The YMCA was a most positive experience for us. Baby Ann was occupying much of Joan's time, while I threw myself into some hard work. The running of the 87-bed hostel was refreshing, after the harshness of youth club work. The clientele covered a spectrum of students and local young men. Some students were on mining courses locally and were working-class kids away from home.

Others were from Iran, Zambia, Oman. Some were unemployed, bored or problematic.

For the first time in my life I had worked in the drug scene in St Helens. We picked up several drug users via our hostel, concerts and 'Fish Rappers', which were music-based 'come and be challenged to think' evenings. It makes me feel good to think back to those days and remember the young men and women who fell in love with Jesus and decided to let him influence their lives.

Even though I ran lots of evangelistic events and large rock concerts, as well as the hostel, Joan and I still look back at those two years as a healthy break between 'Y' Club and Mayflower. Joan was in good health and we both enjoyed our work. We loved the people and they loved us. It was heartbreaking to leave – but God had called us to London's East End to a life we didn't know existed. If I had known the pain ahead I believe I would never have chosen to go.

Chapter 2

References

1. Jim Wallis, *The Call to Conversion* (Lion 1981).

3: Axe holes in the door

I remember well leaving St Helens YMCA with tears in our eyes. The YMCA family had taken us warmly into their lives. The grandads in the snooker room right next to our first floor flat loved our little girls, now aged one and seven years old. The 200 pensioners in the lunch club responded generously to my rather loud humour and often repeated one-liner jokes. Now, in January 1975, following the removal van down the M1 in our blue caravanette, we were entering a new life for our family, and a new kind of youth work.

I was struck first by the sheer ugliness of the club building. I would describe it now as non-shalom. (Shalom is a Hebrew word meaning peace, but also with implications of wholeness and completeness; I will discuss it again later.) Outside it looked like a square lump of concrete – no windows and steel-lined front doors. I know now why there were hammer and axe holes on the front door of the club. It was non-shalom.

Inside it was painted almost entirely in some horrible green gloss paint that had been donated to Mayflower. It gave me and, I am sure, the members a distinct institutional feeling. This, coupled with the long Pentonville-type corridors, with solid locked doors on both sides gave me a trapped, oppressive feel. It was totally depressing. What sort of kids can come in here and enjoy it? What does this place *do* to kids? It was so disheartening and yet it challenged me to change it. (Eventually I had most of it painted matt black and bought a lorry load of green fluorescent tubes and colourful pop music and Christian posters.) It had been built for relief work in the 1930s, and on top of that it was really beaten up. Yet it was big – so big that it had two coffee bars, two gyms and a large outdoor football court, an air rifle range, snooker room and boxing room. There were numerous other activity rooms in various states of disorder including one full of four foot high blocks of Scalextrix car racing track. Another sported a new disco unit and sound system.

One of the few pieces of equipment that was available in the open club was a table-tennis table with a plank of wood nailed across it instead of a net. As two kids played another walked across 'the net'.

I make recordings of my evenings in club. I can look back now at my notes from my very first night in the club:

Some friendly contact and interest in my arrival, some busy and interested in football outside, plus snooker, table-tennis. Some silly, bored kids messing about – boys barricaded themselves in the beat-up room and then smashed down the panelled walls to get out. Others jumped over canteen trying to nick sweets and money. Remember a few names. Ro' a black kid, Maria and Carol (bandaged arm), Jim, Skunkie . . . little kids running. Several groups around – girls *standing*! Building far too rambling and terrible to supervise – leaders just policing. Activities severely limited. Conclusion – No one focal point. No warmth of atmosphere – although some residents have good relationships with kids. Great need for positive activity and discipline boundaries.

Decisions—redesign toilets, block main corridor, move all refreshments to coffee bar—ONE FOCAL POINT, develop office . . .

I notice in my second evenings recordings that 'Carol's arm is now unbandaged'. That sort of detailed observation is important in youth work. The recording of it helps to concrete it in the mind alongside many other personal detail relevant to *them*. Even now, ten years later, I can remember that Carol, now a local mum with two kids, once had an injured arm. It makes me smile to think of approaching her ten years later and asking if her arm is better! But the point is that the first duty of love is to listen. Listen with your eyes.

There was much love practised at this level of youth work —but what did the kids do in club? For a start, try to imagine holding back up to a hundred kids who want to get in quickly, mostly without paying their 5p. 'Steaming the door' meant a lot to most youth workers at Mayflower over the years. First interactions were always hostile, and conflict had to be used as a starting point for relationships. We started the evening with at least three of the biggest male team members manning the door. I still have the 'reception sheets' from those early days and the first dozen names who came in were always the biggest and toughest. Now in their late twenties, most of them are professional criminals in or out of prison.

A typical evening might be like this. The oldest and toughest, the eighteen and nineteen-year-olds, took their choice of football pitch. In good weather it would be the outside yard, otherwise they opted for the cage gym, a converted theatre only useful for mad games. The slightly younger toughest opted for the top gym and football there. The youngest males, aged fourteen and fifteen, headed for the beat-up room, which was equipped with ropes and cushions from old settees, and let go their energy and aggression by beating each other up. Youth workers often joined in and it was a great place for making contact (and collecting a bloody nose!). The table-tennis table as described, and a large snooker table with slashed cloth satisfied some. Mostly they came, I think, to enjoy and meet with others, get rid of energy and bait the middleclass workers!

Amongst all this some workers had developed wholesome relationships with some kids. Little groups of kids came in to do various activities and discovered real love from people who came from very different cultural backgrounds.

My second night in club was my big showdown and I had to be rescued by John Bourne who had been acting leader before I came. Young fifteen-year-old Johnny had handed his knife in and at the end of club he demanded it back. My reasonable suggestion of handing it back at the door on the way out was met by my first confrontation, and it shook me to the roots. Such power, will, determination, psychological dominance and aggression! In ten years full-time youth work I had never met such psychologically strong kids. There were many more such confrontations to be experienced.

As well as individuals in club we also had gangs with names. In 1975 'The Snipers' were a gang who dominated club. They were all seventeen to nineteen-year-old boys who were notorious in the community and much wider afield. They were pub and street fighters, football supporters of the violent kind, and Mayflower was *their* club.

There were many positives about them. They loved good times and had lots of 'real characters' among them with genuine humour. There was also a whole range of skills and trades represented. The real hard men, the expert 'cat burglar', the quick thief, the quiet handler of stolen goods –

the gang could do anything. They were planners and sophisticated. They were also cocky cockneys!

Doug, one of my colleagues, tells of one of his first experiences of taking The Snipers out in the minibus on an ice-skating trip. Approaching the car park and the single arm barrier, Jimmy said, 'hang on', jumped out of the bus and broke off the barrier like a matchstick.

One member wrote this poem, which will give an idea of the image they hoped to project:

THE SNIPERS POEM

Oh, to be a Sniper,
To be feared far and wide,
To be on the dole for all my life,
To even go inside.

I'd walk around Canning Town,
Right stroppy like you'll know,
I'd never smile or be kind,
Cos toughness and niceness don't go.

I'd scare the wits out of everyone,
I'd make them really spit,
I would be the top man,
I really would be it.

We have got no leader,
What would we do with one,
If anyone tried to rule us,
We'd get him with a gun.

The Snipers are the bravest,
The Snipers are the greatest,
If you mess around,
Then they really put you underground.

I don't want you to think I am exaggerating or confused due to a ten year time lag. I've always recorded on paper the activities, incidents and people and these help me to give an authentic account now. One particular evening, I went home late after club and spoke into a tape recorder. The purpose was to give the Christian Publicity Organisation an idea of our situation at Mayflower, as they were producing material for us. But I started off by telling them of that particular evening's club . . .

I have just got in from club, and just to put you in the atmosphere tonight, we had all the members come in, and a big gang from the club called 'The Snipers', and every one of them was armed. Some had hammers, some had breadknives, and one had a bayonet, one an axe; others had all sorts of 'tools' as they call them. They came into club, paid their subs. I was on the door and didn't see one of them with a tool, and yet when they were inside they were brandishing them, flick-knives and breadknives . . . They stayed for an hour, and then they went down to the local fun fair to 'fight the blacks'. It isn't unusual, of course, to have this sort of trouble; we have run trips to football matches and people have got stabbed, and we've had fights in the club, and three weeks ago someone faintly resembling a 'Paki' got beat up just outside the entrance. And all these are members. Not that I'm bragging about it – because I am ashamed. But it is people who are real, real members, real Canning Town kids – and we work with them.

It is absolutely horrible to work with them, love them, and yet see the sorts of things they do. We work with them all the time, and it makes you so sad.

The last time we were open before tonight was

Friday. They were talking about how the night before they had jumped on a little Pakistan boy at the same fun fair. Only little, nothing to fight against really, and yet they jumped up and down on him, on his face, so that the blood spurted out.

What we have to offer in club, the games and facilities, cannot compete with the thrill and kicks they get out of the violence which makes us feel repulsed, and yet to them is the really exciting thing in life.

When all the lads went out we decided as leaders to do something that we had never done before – because it was such a dangerous situation. We phoned the 'Old Bill' (the police, that is) anonymously, and told them that there was a big gang, armed up to their eye-balls, on their way to the fun fair. The 'blacks' did not turn up and the Old Bill actually nicked one of the lads for carrying a breadknife. All the rest of them came back having got rid of their energies in a way, just the tension of doing that sort of thing. They enjoyed it.

One of our other members got stabbed during the evening, in the arm, but we don't know the whole story.

I am telling you this really so that it will fill you in with what is happening night after night, and facing this tension night after night by going into club is my problem. So many kids you have an incredible relationship with; others you do not. And if they carry a knife it is very difficult to lovingly discipline them, and still keep a relationship. I hope you will pray with us in this. It is such a burden.

Just tonight I was talking to one of the girls. She and her boyfriend are both regular members, but he was picked up a week ago in an armed robbery (he's only seventeen), and I was telling her how I had written to

Billy and sent him some comic strip booklets. She said she thought they were good. When we sent them to Borstal, everyone reads them, not just one lad.

Late on, when the lads came back from the fairground battles, they were picking up literature. One, called Shorty (whose probation officer is a Christian) was reading *Run Baby, Run* and he was very interested; I told him that it was a true story. One of the other lads said he'd seen the film. When we turned the lights off at the end of the club, one of the lads swore and ran to the bar where there were lights so that he could carry on reading – and this is what happens with something that is readable.

The first year and more was full of incidents like the ones just described in the club.

From my side there was physical change in club, more direct Christian input from films, visiting speakers, Christian posters, comics etc. These regular inputs were supplemented by irregular special evangelistic efforts. Alongside this was a whole social education of films, discussion and, of course, stretching physical activities. There was lots of interaction between all of us with attendances running up to 100 each night.

These lads were difficult to communicate with. They kenw little about Christianity and tended to treat Christians with coolness and suspicion. But one of the most effective ways we found of stimulating and challenging the kids, and communicating the gospel to them, was the 'Ten o'clock Newz'. This was something established at the 'Y' Club to provide some Christian thought-provoking stimulus to the kids, and we introduced it to Mayflower.

Ten o'clock Newz was held at 9.50 pm in Senior Club.

All machines: pin-ball, video, juke box etc. were turned off and lights dimmed. Kids were encouraged to come in to the Coffee Bar, and most did, rather than continue table-tennis and other sports or go home.

The speaker stood in a central raised position and spot-lighted, using the microphone to communicate. The message had to have real impact and relevance to the kids' lives if they were to listen. We told our speakers to keep it very short — unless the kids were obviously gripped.

Response was sometimes shouts and abuse from a minority or sometimes comments from the floor, which could be used to build on the message.

We have had some incredible times at Ten o'clock Newz — and, of course, many disasters. The kids, generally speaking, love it. 'What's on Newz tonight, Pip?' they would say towards the end of the evening and a good discussion would often result from just that. Sometimes a theme would run for weeks and the kids would continue the debate in every corner of the club. Jesus must be news to our kids. Good News too.

One particularly effective method of helping young people to know where they are in relationship to God is the Football Pitch[1].

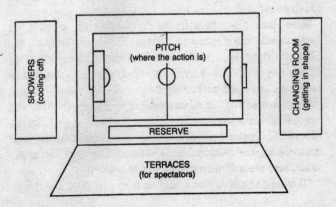

SHOWERS (cooling off)

PITCH (where the action is)

CHANGING ROOM (getting in shape)

RESERVE

TERRACES (for spectators)

Hanging on the Mayflower club wall is half a table-tennis table painted white with this diagram drawn on it. The question is: Where are you on the pitch? Where are you in relationship to God?

– are you on the *terraces*, just a spectator?
– are you in the *changing rooms* getting ready for action?
– are you perhaps even closer to God, on the *reserve bench*?
– or are you a Christian, on *the pitch* – where the action is?

Others may place themselves in *the showers* – cooling off from the action of being a Christian. Some youth workers have placed themselves here – feeling tired, battered, soiled and needing refreshment before returning to the pitch.

In the club, during Ten o'clock Newz this pitch has been used to get kids to think and publicly declare where they are. I always remember Ingrid, one of our beautiful black girls, walking from the disco area across the social area to place herself on the terraces. Others have said, 'I'm in the pub on the corner of the next street!' or, 'I'm on the terraces with my back to the pitch!' (That says a lot, doesn't it?) Bones, an eighteen-year-old boy, placed himself on the terraces, but a week later in the midst of a chat pointed out that he had moved to the changing rooms – getting ready!

This device is used a lot in the youth club to make it easier to talk about Christian things. Kids easily respond or bring up the subject without any feeling of threat. Among Christians it is also a very useful device for cultivating spiritual self-disclosure. Often in our full-timers' daily 'Feelings Meeting' (a share and prayer time together) we ask, 'Where are you on the pitch at the moment?' 'I'm on the pitch – the touch line, but no one is passing me the ball,' said a keen Christian. What does that say? Here are other responses I've heard during the years:

'I'm on the pitch, but lying on a stretcher.'

'I'm on the pitch, but with shins bleeding, playing defence all the time.'

'I'm scoring goals!'

'Mid-field distributing the ball and keeping abreast of the game.'

'I'm dirty, knackered, sweaty – but I'm on the pitch.'

In the *Rolling Magazine* Fun Tent that I head up at Greenbelt Christian Arts Festival every year, 'The Pitch' is used effectively to cultivate sharing in small groups as well as to challenge the known Christian celebrities and artistes.

In the club, nasty incidents continued to happen. A resident had his hair set on fire, a radiator was pulled from the wall and the club flooded while a chair was set on fire at the same time. The kids physically harassed workers and I had to develop new skills of responding physically too, but in a non-threatening manner. Sometimes in the early days when I was being verbally abused I used to give the boy a sharp kick in the shins and smile. It was usually unseen by his mates and yet it was felt by the offending young man with positive results. I would be criticised by many for this sort of action and I wouldn't do it now, but it did get results and respect in those early days of 'Who's that fat slob with the funny voice?'

This links with what I now call 'Get lost theology'. Let me illustrate. During 1984 we had a great deal of disruption and physical attacks from a gang called 'the Smithys'. They had 'steamed' the club, swinging iron bars and broken cues, attacking kids and youth workers. Some time later they turned up when Margaret and Deb were on the door. 'Can I nip upstairs and get a light for my fag?' said one infamous member of the gang who was currently charged with burglary and arson – burning down a local corner shop. 'Get lost!' said Deb, 'I'll get one for you.' Three years before that, she would have let him in, with the whole gang, and it would have been goodbye quiet evening! The 'Get lost theology' is basically being wise enough not to get conned.

Patrick Butler, one of our long-term workers, who has now left us for a professional Youth and Community Work training, speaks of his most memorable lesson which happened early during his Mayflower time:

Oddball, Murph, Pete, Micky and a few others chatting were with me by the coffee bar. Murph pulled me aside and whispered something in my ear. 'Ask Micky how his mum dances.' I was reluctant, feeling very unsure of my ground, but not wanting to appear a spoilsport. His persistence soon won over my uncertainty and I asked Micky how his mum danced. A deathly hush fell amongst the group and Micky grabbed me and thrust me against the wall. I heard murmurs of 'the bastard!', and 'fancy asking him *that*'. Micky, with a fist held close to my face warned me colourfully and in no uncertain terms what would happen to me if I ever said anything like that again, and it was only when he let me go and I backed off shaken and confused that Murph explained that Micky's mum was in a wheelchair and hadn't got any legs!

It was just a 'wind-up', as it is known in Canning Town.

A teenager approaches me in club and says, 'Pip, I want to become a Christian.' 'Get lost,' I say. That has happened *so often*. That question, the most incredible, exciting question a person can ask, and yet I say 'get lost'. The reason is that you become culturally aware, and therefore understand what they are *really* saying, gaining respect in the process. Otherwise you are written off as a 'wally', as Patrick described in another incident.

One evening I got talking to Kev and a few of his mates. Kev told me he was unemployed and we talked for a long time about how he felt about not being able to get a job. He described his frustrations, staying in bed until lunch-time, having no money. My heart went out to him. I therefore felt humiliated when later I discovered that Kev in fact did have a job and that our whole conversation had just been a joke.

Another wind-up!

'Get lost theology' means loving kids so much that you learn how to communicate within *their* culture. When someone *really* asks how you become a Christian, 'Get lost' is never the reply!

This 'Get lost theology' can also be reversed and the kids themselves develop a 'rubbish philosophy'. I can remember someone fifteen years ago coming up to me after a Ten o'clock Newz at the 'Y' Club and saying 'That what you said was a load of rubbish.' What he was really saying was, 'Tell me more about Jesus.' *It was a question!* An aggressive approach that was followed by an earnest conversation about Jesus. That night the young man believed that Jesus followed him home as he walked the dark streets. Some days later he committed his life to his Creator as we sat at the club coffee bar together. That same 'Rubbish' approach has been made to me much more recently at the Mayflower too.

During 1984 we had a particularly difficult boy who came into club on his own, but attached himself to the most troublesome gang at that time. He was about sixteen, well-built and very well dressed, like all of the kids. His particular behaviour was not only being abusive, throwing chips, bashing equipment etc., but also deliberately approaching leaders and challenging them to physical confrontation. He used to approach Patrick, who himself is young and physically fit, and push him and kick him to force some reaction from him. Often I had to have eyes in the back of my head to be able to intervene and place my older, less muscular, and less threatening frame between them. He would never disclose his name to us. He signed in as Donald Duck or the current most popular West Ham player, so when we talked about him in the de-brief meetings after club we used to call him '£98 Jumper'. That was because the only disclosure he had made about himself was that his sweater had cost £98.

One disco night he was being particularly obnoxious and, praying the club through — as you *have* to do for safety and sanity — I spied my chance. I was pushing my way through the crush near the coffee bar and £98 Jumper was perched on the side of a seating module. As I went past I punched him in the testicles, paused briefly, smiled and walked on. It hurt him, I could tell. He said nothing then, but later on the next evening he was in, and he took trouble to chat with me. It was a stand-up chat giving him the chance to discontinue the conversation at his will, yet he disclosed much of his life that night, about his school experiences, home, friends, clothes, in fact it was a breakthrough. I had made contact with him. Physical contact that demanded to be noticed. This was surrounded by love, warmth, smiles and appropriately shown willingness to talk.

You don't handle everyone in that way, in fact, that was unusual. Sometimes you let things go because there are more important priorities. In that first year, in 1975, I wrote in my Youth Report: 'As I walked past a corridor in club last week two teenage boys were fighting with knives and I just walked on by. It was a friendly fight. A few seconds later I paused, "What am I doing?" Here am I getting conditioned into the ways I know to be wrong . . .'

A typical response from people who hear about these sort of incidents would be, 'Does the club *create* these sort of incidents and thereby these sort of young people?'

I always say Mayflower is unique – not one of many similar organisations, but grown up from interacting with Canning Town people and aiming at meeting their needs. While all this was happening in club, our community, the London Borough of Newham, was being statistically and negatively described like this:

Highest crime rate in the country
London's most deprived borough
Education priority area
Socially deprived area
Highest unemployment among young people in London
Highest number of tower blocks in the country
Lowest education results in the country
Least number of trees in the country
Largest housing waiting list

A leaflet handed out on the local Rathbone market in 1975 claimed that, 'Newham people suffer more illness and die earlier than in any other part of the country.'

With all this as a back drop, is it any wonder that the kids' behaviour spilled over in club? Our job was about intervening in their lives. They are valuable, incredible young people, who suffered from being devalued and disregarded. They were loved and they didn't know that they were loved so much that Jesus had already died for them. They didn't know that, even if they responded to Jesus and became Christians, God wouldn't love them any more than He does already. (He would be very pleased though!)

Being involved in these extreme incidents doesn't mean that these kids are any greater sinners than suburban youngsters, or people from the most upper-class homes. It means that on top of their own personal sin, which we all suffer from, they also suffer from *social sin*. The sin that society imposes upon them. The same sin and injustice that is starving millions of Ethiopians to death.

It costs to love – because love isn't a plaque you hang on a wall, it is something you *do* to people.

Chapter 3

References

1. Lyman Coleman and Denny Rydberg, *Knowing me: On my identity* (Scripture Union 1982).

4: Working with gangs

It had always been normal for many of our teenage boys to carry knives. One club evening we noticed other 'tools' beginning to be smuggled into club. Sticks, some with nails protruding, iron bars and hammers. At the same time, sticks, stones and bottles were being hidden outside the building ready for the end of the club evening. The 'Tramps' gang were preparing for battle.

'The Snipers' gang numbered only a few now. Much work had been done with them over the years – their own Sunday club with their own bank account; holidays; weekends; many court appearances. Now they came into club irregularly. 'The Minis' gang, from a past of disruption, were maturing and were now less disruptive, but well-prepared to do battle with the hyperactive, disruptive, violent 'Tramps' gang. It was becoming a regular occurrence for the Tramps to attack and bait the Minis, concluding in a street battle at closing time – with sticks, bricks and bottles being thrown.

It became so bad that we shut the club for ten days to cool off. One evening, as the workers met to pray and discuss the strategy for the future, the meeting was 'steamed'. Forty or so kids came in and all of a sudden it became a meeting, with Denny and Jimmy, two older boys, taking the chair between them. I facilitated the meeting but in no way was I in control. First of all they 'slagged off' me and the other workers for running a lousy club—'You can't handle it'—and then they turned on the Tramps and ran their own Kangaroo Court.

One particular exchange between Jimmy, Denny and one of the Tramps stood out clearly to me as I recorded it on paper the same evening:

Jimmy: You think you're hard! Anybody can pick on Christians! Christians are robots. They don't wanna fight. Why don't you pick on niggers with knives? You're soft. Laying into Christians ain't on—it's your club. Use your head. Nobody else will have you. Anyway, the Tramps aren't even thieves . . .

Phil: Yeah, we are.

Denny: Who said that? No, you're not thieves, you're kids . . .

Jimmy: Yeah, you think that nicking half a dozen Granny Smiths off the market and going getting the teas in at Bianci's Café is real hard . . .

Phil: No, we go real thieving . . .

Jimmy: Oh, so you've graduated to Golden Delicious, have you?

After the 'slagging off' came the verdict. 'Stay away,' said Jimmy, 'stay away for a year from now. You're barred and if you roll up you're nicked!' That was authority speaking and the workers' meeting that eventually took place that evening affirmed that decision. The Tramps were barred from club for a year, the first time that a long term suspension had been imposed. It wasn't left like that, but we decided to work with the Tramps outside the club. Not reject them but, with love and commitment, intensify our youth work with them.

Two of our team members were chosen to head up the

group work with me in support. Alan Garthwaite was in his late twenties, a working-class Londoner, and came to us from a drug rehabilitation centre. He was maintenance man at Mayflower and a natural for making warm contact with kids. Dave Seamark was a contrast to Alan. He too lived in the Mayflower hostel, but was from a middle-class background and studying to be a doctor. He had a keen sense of humour and lots of enthusiasm. Both of them were committed Christians and threw themselves into working regularly with this gang.

At the same time as we were handling all this within our own unit, I was making contact and seeking co-operation from other agencies. Resulting from these efforts I called a case conference at Mayflower between probation officers, other youth workers, police inspectors, social workers, Kris Traer (my first full-time permanent colleague), my other colleagues and myself.

Collecting all the facts about the Tramps was a major item. These kids were indiscriminately disruptive – smashing up the local school youth centre, 'doing' shops and the Jobcentre in a similar way. In fact, the day before this case conference, a number of the gang had been nicked in the market area for disrupting the Jobcentre, and the court had them 'bound over to keep the peace'. Other incidents had been reported: two shops had been raided; other shop windows smashed; fights in a local pub; complaints from local people about late night vandalism and abuse. There was clearly much concern in the community. The conclusion of the meeting was to adopt a co-ordinated approach in which each agency used its particular skills and facilities for intervention. Intervention that was not just for the community's benefit alone, but for the growth and development of these precious teenagers. The development we looked for was not to result in hardening them, but in releasing them, which I believe is what the Good News is about.

A local probation officer said at this time, 'We only respond to situations in our profession; you (as a voluntary community-based organisation) are able to take initiatives.'

God took the initiative when He loved the world, so much that He sent Jesus to live and then die on the cross for us. That is why Christians just cannot lie back and let the world destroy itself. We need to model ourselves on Jesus Himself—and get involved as He did. And it costs, folks!

The Tramps at this time were approximately twenty strong, but there were others who attached themselves to the gang for certain activities. Only the hard core were barred for the year and worked with as a group. The remainder continued as members of the club four evenings a week and were involved in other miscellaneous activities.

Things continued to happen quickly. Certain gang members were arrested for burglary and other offences. Others were sent to detention centre and Borstal for crimes committed a year before.

Seven of the hard core remained for us to work with outside the club, which we did by using the club minibus as a mobile group room.

The first request from the boys was to drive around the Isle of Dogs. This was considered to be 'extending their new experiences' and yet it was less than one mile from Canning Town. After this they decided to venture further afield.

I gave support, encouragement, direction and prayed with Dave and Alan, but they did the work. Dave recorded his experiences at this time.

One evening we went to Epping Forest and there played wide-games. The lads really enjoyed this but we learned one thing, that Spiff and a number of others were afraid of the dark! I had a camera with me that evening and this was a great help in breaking down barriers. Spiff proved to be quite photogenic.

After the success of the Epping Forest trip, we were looking forward to greater things. We decided to take a drive in the minibus to Richmond. The minibus provides a sanctuary for its occupants from which they can give forth verbal abuse. This evening was no exception and when we were stuck in a traffic jam the abuse, particularly towards black people, reached a climax. Spiff and another boy spat into the faces of a black couple in an adjacent car. A very ugly scene resulted with the black man rightly incensed and wishing to spread all of us out on Hammersmith Broadway. Of our brave little group nothing was to be seen; they were too busy trying to crawl under the seats . . . The situation was diffused by Alan's timely intervention, diplomacy and above all, God's Holy Spirit working through him.

We drove home in silence. The lads were shocked and stunned especially by the fact that I had received the blow meant for them. As they climbed out of the bus, Spiff put his hand on my shoulder and apologised. It was then I could see some truth in the well-used quotation, 'We know that in all things God works for good with those who love him, who are called according to his purpose' (Rom. 8:28).

Since then, our relationship with Spiff has been noticeably different – still boisterous, playful and abusive, but the signs of friendship are present. Confidences are being exchanged; we have met his family; invited him into Mayflower; begun to love. We plan to start canoeing with four of the boys this year and they are enthusiastic to say the least. Every evening we spend with them means one less chance of them being involved in a robbery or getting drunk, means we learn more about life in Canning Town, means one more opportunity for them to meet with Christians on their own terms and we believe, brings them nearer to life in all its fullness – knowledge of Jesus Christ.

We had great plans for the group as you see. The reality was much slower, and we had to meet the Tramps where they were. We had real problems of limiting the group to seven core members. They were so attractive to the rest of the peer group. We also had problems actually keeping this hard gang out of the club. They were forever breaking into the club from all directions, as well as physically 'steaming' the front door. The police were called regularly as the whole team were under stress. The dark, cold winter nights didn't help. There was little else for the kids to do – at least the police and the Mayflower provided some excitement in a drab community and bored lives.

This type of work wasn't the only type of group work being done at the Mayflower. This work was particularly geared to meet the needs of the hard-core Tramps. You can't have a curriculum and dish it out like a Sunday school lesson book. The kids don't just sit down and respond to *our* programming. Developmental group work can take several forms.

The Chuck group was formed because a number of Inter Club boys (aged around fourteen) wouldn't come up into Senior Club. Two workers, Pete Oliver and Pete Smith, worked closely with them and even though leaders changed slowly over the five years a continuity remained. The group decided its own programme, planned its own holidays and events. These voluntary youth workers shared their lives (and obviously that means their faith in Jesus) with these kids. Several times we called in our friends' Christian lawyer, Tim, who helped and advised the group in their 'social affairs'. There is a bookful of interest in this group alone – but there have been others . . .

Two local mums, Marion and Michele, started 'M' group, which catered mainly for girls. Charlie and Piff worked with a group of local boys who are now mostly professional criminal men – they were a tough group as kids. S.P.L.K. girls' group started with Joyce and Joy in response to a spoken Christian need. Ali and Andy led another group also with a definite Christian content. This was a mixed group who pursued a regular Bible-based programme. Doug and Deb did years of work with another mixed group. Jeannie and I worked with a girls' group, Andy and I with Aggro group, Rob and I with the Nillies and so on.

Some of our groups have been recognised during the years by I.T. (Intermediate Treatment) which, under the auspices of Social Services, aims to help settle young offenders whilst keeping them in the community.

In recent years two additional groups have been formed from young people in early adolescence, all of whom made a formal Christian commitment before the group work commenced. They have the journey of adolescence before them: sexual encounters, drugs, booze, crime, relationship conflicts, unemployment . . . I am a realistic Christian with 'hope', not an optimist! I always remember being at a wedding and having some men say to me, 'We used to be Christians – got confirmed, holidays, Bible studies and all that, but we gave it up; we couldn't keep it up *and* have a good time!'

Each group was conducted with great love and concern

for the wholeness of young people. Each one was as professionally run as possible; each one as explicitly Christian as appropriate. Some wouldn't recognise the 'Christian' content. They were often not 'paper Bible' based, but 'concrete'.

I met with all the group workers fortnightly if possible. We talked through the group life and the maintenance of its 'boundaries'. We have always operated Boundary Management, which entailed the least change as possible to things like membership, leadership, times and location. We prayed and planned and responded flexibly to the changing needs of these special kids. We often tried to let them 'set the agenda'.

Soon after our second case conference we had several bad incidents where, to add to the disruption, workers were attacked in a nasty way. Pat and Darren entered the Mayflower during the day and made an unprovoked, serious attack on Alan, which necessitated hospital attention. We were forced to bring in the police and prosecute. It was a hard decision, as a Christian Family Centre committed to bringing Good News to the poor in spirit, to bring in the police to prosecute the kids we were actually loving in Jesus' name.

Alan, too, had great inner conflicts. His own bad experiences with police, courts and prison, from his drug dependency days, made it very difficult for him to decide to go ahead. I wrote at the time:

> The team decided for Pat's own good that we needed to face him with his own behaviour by prosecuting him. It wasn't easy as the police offered little support. We found it extremely difficult to get the police to charge Pat for this vicious attack. Alan suffered from slight

concussion for some time afterwards and considerable emotional stress. Pat was held in an assessment centre until he was eventually given a detention centre sentence. I knew several of his family – relationships were stretched considerably. His older brother, Johnny, wrote from prison and reassured me. 'My brother is a pain in the neck, but don't worry, he will soon grow up.' Johnny didn't reject me, but welcomed my ongoing contact with him while in prison. To write and to visit prison is so time consuming, and yet so positive in building relationships from initial superficial contact. His mum didn't think much of me. *I* was the pain in the neck and it was me who was blamed for pressing charges against Pat. I became unwelcome at the home and relationships cooled.

Then one day a letter from Johnny: 'I'm up at the Bailey on Monday.' I was with him right away. It is always a fearful experience for me to be down in those cells at the Old Bailey Central Criminal Court, and *I* was only visiting and counselling. But it was terrific also to get alongside Johnny and Pat's mum too. She was present, with the co-defendant's mum, and sharing their nervous energy and a pint in the pub at lunch-time helped heal the soured relationship. It was later that week, following the guilty verdict, that I had to speak to the court. Before the sentence the judge listens to any character reference to decide on the level of criminality. At that time I wrote in my report about that experience:

Because of the obvious behaviour change that we had seen in Johnny, although certainly not a non-offender, I could speak very well of him before the court. The battle was Borstal or an alternative! Having already completed a D.C. in his early teens, the alternatives seemed few. The judge, however, listened, like no other I have experienced, and gave Johnny only a deferred sentence of six months 'to prove himself'. There followed a time of confusion in court after his sentence because of the complication of Johnny being in custody for another offence. The sentence was changed to being 'bound over for two years to keep the peace on a sum of £10'. A very lenient sentence for a high court.

This 'Borstal or not' debate is an ongoing one! (Borstal is now called Youth Custody.) My latest figures show a failure rate of 83% (within two years) at a cost of £231 per week. What good does Youth Custody do? The choice for Johnny was to put him in a place where he could fraternise with a selected bunch of professional criminals, where he could learn the 'business' and yet make no decisions about his own life . . . or keep him in the community where at least there are *some* non-offenders, and where he can make decisions (and mistakes) and come to terms with his life.

The Chief Constable of Greater Manchester was quoted in the press as saying that criminals should be punished, 'with the severity such conduct merits until they mend their ways'. Is that the Christian response? It seems so sad to me that a civilised society has got to cage its young people instead of 'treating' them. Treatment at Mayflower, we estimate, costs us only £70 per head per year, and yet the numbers of young people being institutionalised is rising.

It seems, however, that those who are 'punished' return to society and continue to commit *the majority* of crimes. A local Detective Sergeant said to me recently, 'I don't think about what happens to them once they are inside – and what they do when they come out – I just nick them.' Who *does* think? If we in the community don't these kids will just go in and out of the custody machine like sausages! So little effort is put into prevention. If we are not part of the solution, then we are part of the problem!

In fact, Johnny had to return to remand centre awaiting trial at Snaresbrook Crown Court on his burglary charge. He wrote from his cell: 'Thanks for what you said at the Old Bailey . . . what you said I couldn't quite hear all of it because the screw was speaking . . . the worst thing about being here is the night because you are banged up from about 4.30 pm till about 7.45 am which drives me mad . . .'

That spurred me once again. 'The spirit of the Lord is upon me . . . because he has chosen me to bring good news to the poor, he has sent me to proclaim liberty to the captives . . . to set free the oppressed . . .' (Luke 4:18-19) and Johnny was poor, captive and oppressed. I saw him as a damaged child, created by God, contaminated by his own wrongs, other people's wrongs, communal wrongs and the hard-heartedness of the educated. Johnny is a living example of someone who was experiencing 'a poverty that imprisons the spirit'.[1]

Not only was Johnny experiencing poverty of spirit, but also physical incarceration. The damage that is done by locking someone up like a wild animal is unbearable to think about when you love that person. It has a devastating effect! I will never forget reading of the experiment conducted in 1972 in Stanford University, USA. This experiment involved a mock-up of a prison to test different individual responses to the rôles they were asked to play.

All participants were college students or professors and extreme personality types were excluded from the experiment. After only six days (out of a projected fourteen), the experiment had to be stopped because all of those involved, both the keepers and the kept, were suffering severe psychological side-effects. This was simply an experiment, conducted by reasonable, well-educated people who knew that it was only an experiment. It did not even begin to approach the reality of imprisonment as it is known by thousands of human beings in America every day.[2]

Imprisonment, it seems to me, needs to be used only for serious violent offenders and the severely disturbed. Not for Johnny and his many friends who will be returning to their community trained *only* in more professional ways of committing crime.

John McVicar says, speaking from his own experience, that prison 'breeds aggression . . . The ultimate madness of all these places is that the inmates are allowed to interact with each other in accordance with the same anti-social values which provide the same motive power for crime outside prison.'[3]

After five months of being 'banged up', Johnny was given a Borstal sentence. Eighteen months later, he came out of Borstal, and on his first night out he was arrested for being drunk and smashing up the local café.

Johnny came to terms with the institution OK – he hadn't come to terms with his own community.

The work with the Tramps remained difficult. We still aimed to create some group cohesion via the minibus journeys. The Tramps' self-programming didn't seem to work, but group worker initiatives failed similarly! Even weekends away in Wales failed to create a stable consistent group. Many of our workers continued to do detached youth work during this time and the contact was valuable with many young people. Homes were visited, but as the months passed we still felt that we hadn't 'cracked it'. Then, one day a group of college students appeared in the community looking for a group of teenagers to work on a video film-making project. This was in no way meant to be a Tramps project, but they grabbed the equipment in the local park and just took over! We had a few disastrous sessions as the students became acclimatised to our 'cultural norms', but then the group settled into the project on their chosen topic – The National Front.

It was done! The video was completed and then the group disintegrated. It seemed that some learning and satisfaction had been achieved. A number of hard-core members were 'inside'. Three others were picked up within another of our I.T. groups, and others started serious courting. The whole process of group work with that one gang lasted seven months. Considerable time has passed since then, but contacts remain. How good was the work? How effective? The Lord knows the Good News reflected in the twinkling eyes and smiles of Christian workers. The Lord knows the practical love expressed in difficult circumstances, and the wet-eyed prayers, prayed into the dark winter nights.

One major difficulty was that we had very little support and the organisational structure came only from our own unit. The Social Services department and Intermediate Treatment Unit gave us no financial support, and there was no real co-ordinated approach from professionals even though we have always had exceptionally good relationships with the probation service. The Church has remained largely indifferent.

During this time other things were happening in our lives. At the same time as the work with the Tramps and the other youth work, we were realising the vision of a new club. Women and men of Canning Town were working and praying towards new buildings that visibly demonstrated Good News. We believed our work was being done in Jesus' name and to the best of our ability.

The whole of the Mayflower was to be redeveloped. Under the leadership of Roger Sainsbury, Mark Birchall, Rich Gerrard and other special visionaries, the £1 million project went forward as a massive step of faith. The Mayflower 'flock' not only worked hard but supported the youth work in every possible way.

Much earlier, in 1959, the Albemarle Report on the Youth Service had been published. It highlighted the fact that much youth work was taking place, 'in surroundings whose dinginess suggest relief work in the thirties'. How that reminded me of our own club at Mayflower!

The government responded to that report, launching a Youth Service Building Programme. Kids in Canning Town, however, were left behind. It was not until the mid-1970s that we could escape from our dinginess. We were excited, though, to hear that the borough, Newham, had placed us first on the list for the building programme, which would mean that 75% of the costs of rebuilding would be met.

In a society where the rich get richer and the poor get poorer, I was so looking forward to the day when we would have a purpose-built youth club – purpose-built to help introduce real young people to hope and purpose in life.

These difficult kids need to be valued. They are of value. Jesus died for them – he loves them. Just saying it isn't enough – love has to be practical. John Powell says, 'People do not care how much you know until they know how much you care.'[4] They know we care when it's said and shown. The opposite can do so much damage. I always remember a quote from a social workers' magazine about a detention centre discharge report on a young person, 'The greatest achievement in this boy's life is that he breathes.' Can anyone be that worthless? If the Christian life is about love –and that's why I joined–we need to cancel these negatives in life and replace them by positive and practical love. We need to affirm people and help them to realise how valuable they are–to us and to God.

The building process is a story in itself. The architects came into club and asked the kids *their* opinions! The furnishing stages, carpet, seating, colour-scheme were all debated with our senior members over the months. They felt they had some responsibility for their club. While work on the club was only in progress, visitors were impressed by the quality of work, by the design, even by the atmosphere already evident.

We opened on 28 January 1980, though some parts of the club were still unfinished. It was like discovering a new planet. At last we had a well-designed and well-built building which we believed was an extension of God's creativity. We felt it would give us a solid base for the work we were doing with the kids. A new building wouldn't rid them of their frustrations or even get them a job, but it *would* give them a sense of being valued. I believe that a building can help very much to satisfy the needs of our delinquent membership. I also believe that these Canning Town kids should have the best and not just the 'dog ends'.

The club building even won an architecture award from the Royal Institute of British Architects. Their comment was that 'what had been achieved is a building that fulfils its purpose with panache and vigour'.

The day before we opened we prayed in every room, even the toilets. Our desire was to see *Shalom* in every brick.

Chapter 4

References

1. David Sheppard, Dimbleby Lecture 1984.
2. *New York Times Magazine*, 8 April 1973.
3. John McVicar, *McVicar by Himself* (Arrow 1974/79).
4. John Powell, *The Secret of Staying in Love* (Argos 1974).

5: The police

One day I arrived at the club to be told that Kenny had been looking for me when I had been out. He had come to the Mayflower door 'with tears in his eyes', reported my colleague. He traced me eventually and blurted out what had happened.

As a result of hearing his experience, I wrote this letter to the chief inspector at the local police station:

A group of young men known to me have approached me this afternoon complaining about police harassment at 3.40 pm today at the bus stop on the Barking Road near Bianchi's café. P.C. —— and another officer are quoted as saying, 'We don't want to see your faces on the street. We are going to be kind today – let you off this time, but if we see you again we're going to nick you for anything – threatening behaviour – insulting behaviour!

I really believe that they are telling the truth and they were genuinely upset about the incident.

Would you be good enough to respond to this letter? I would really appreciate your co-operation to enable us all to further better community development around here . . .

Resulting from Kenny's initiative and my letter I had a visit from the chief inspector which resulted in very good liaison. He had seen and spoken to the officer concerned and his explanation was that he'd been 'too long on the D.S.U.' (Divisional Support Unit, which is the local minibus of officers now titled 'Instant Response Unit' – the kids call it 'The Wally Wagon'). 'He's forgotten how to be an ordinary copper, in touch with the community,' the chief inspector said. This procedure seemed to be a very positive way of dealing with police harassment, and directing teenagers towards less criminal activities.

I was sad to hear some little while later that the constable concerned had applied to, and was accepted for, the S.P.G. (Special Patrol Group), which has developed an infamous name for behaviour that seemed to be opposed to community policing.

This case of harassment was *not* isolated. I have a whole file of incidents that were reported to me by our teenage boys, together with details of the names and numbers of the officers involved:

1. Police throwing stink bombs into cells when kids were being held awaiting charges.
2. Police carrying water pistols in D.S.U. vehicles and shooting at teenagers they passed in the street, or spraying them with water from squeezy bottles.
3. Wearing 'funny masks' in vehicles and in police stations, and playing practical jokes on prisoners in the cells.
4. The wearing of little red flags in the caps of officers while on patrol, according to the number of times they have 'nicked' the three most scapegoated teenagers.
5. Throwing cups of water over prisoners when stripped for forensic purposes.
6. Physical blows to those arrested.

You may have difficulty in believing all this, but I have evidence that it is true.

The police were especially abusing the drunk by using drunk charges unjustly, it seems to me. A drink charge was a minor offence and didn't warrant legal aid, so the young person had to handle the court and his defence himself! You can imagine what a mess an inarticulate, nervous, seventeen-year-old would make of this. The police however, trained in court procedures, had their patter ready, and the teenager had no chance unrepresented.

Through the case of McKensie v. McKensie (1970), I discovered a way to provide 'lay assistance' to the client. It seems that when a certain case in history creates a precedent it then becomes law. The precedent was set in 1970 that, 'any person, whether he be professional or not, may attend as a friend of either party, may take notes, may quietly make suggestions and give advice.'[1]

It often happened that I, as a 'McKensie friend', would stand in the dock with my notes, whispering ideas and questions to the youngster as he cross-examined the policeman. Usually the young men began nervously but, with assistance, encouragement and the close proximity of a supportive friend, they always grew in confidence. It was in itself excellent social education and social skills training – but we never won a case. New methods had to be found to fight injustice.

Ian Barcham, one of our young voluntary workers who is now a professional youth worker, went out with the 'Bs' (one of the gangs) on a typical Friday night. These extracts from the recording he made of his experience, will help to catch the atmosphere of inner-city life, and the tensions between the kids and the police.

It was ten past eight and feeling somewhat apprehensive I stepped inside the Royal Oak. Out of the five people there Gary was the only person I knew. He bought me a drink, an orange on the rocks for I had decided that on this occasion, as a matter of principle, I would not drink any alcohol, chiefly so as to have a clear mind at all times!! I hadn't explained previously to Gary why I was there and I now felt the need to explain my presence. We chatted for a while. I felt tense wondering how the Bs would respond to me being there on their evening. . . . The pub gradually filled up – Ken, Dave, Les, Martin, Micky, Eddie, Andy – they were all there. I began to feel more relaxed, though a little reserved. . . . The pub atmosphere was very friendly, jocular, noisy, hot and sweaty. . . . Throughout the evening the atmosphere was relaxed; occasionally there would be a bit of larking around, some shouting, but all in very good humour. Occasionally the Bs would band around together and try to wind each other up. I could sense that the Bs were a 'close-knit' group.

It was getting really hot in the pub and people were standing in the entrance. I went outside and stood on the pavement. 'I wouldn't stand there or the "Fuzz" will 'ave yer.' I pressed the matter. Apparently the police had recently stopped outside and told them all to get inside the pub or else they'd all be done for obstructing the highway (enough to put anyone's back up). Accordingly they'd retreated into the pub.

One thing that struck me during my conversation was the power and authority that the police had. If the police told them to do something they'd do it without question – at least in the presence of an officer. This submission is something I believe the kids have learnt from hard experience. I also believe that it is not always positive. If they showed signs of resisting questioning so much the worse for them. They're helpless and powerless against the police. I believe that this position is completely wrong and dangerous; it's not surprising the kids kick against this so hard, and that there is so much hatred and bitterness against not only the police but any 'body' seen as power and authority. With such authority and control, this power can so easily be abused and I have no doubt from what I've heard that it occurs time and time again. In this kind of situation the kids have to be so careful when coming into contact with the police, as it seems that certain police officers are on the look-out for any reason to pick them up – and particularly the 'known ones', and it would appear that there doesn't even need to be a reason.

Standing in the doorway I saw the 'meat wagon' stop at the traffic lights before going down the road. Seven or eight uniformed faces peered through the van windows in our direction. The kids instinctively retreated, including myself.

It seems that the kids and the police are playing a game of cat and mouse and both parties accept and play their rôle – they've got it in for each other.

Between 10.30 pm and 11 pm the 'meat wagon' must have passed about four or five times; on each occasion the news being spread round the pub. Why were the police keeping such a close eye on the Royal Oak, I wonder? Because they genuinely anticipated trouble? Or looking for the opportunity to start it? I feel that only the police can really answer that.

Whether it was just becoming tense as it was approaching closing time and I somehow anticipated trouble, I don't know, but I felt a growing tension in the pub. People kept looking out to see if the police were around. Some kids had already gone, but there seemed to be some confusion by those remaining about when to leave and where to go. I just hung around.

The road was clear so Andy, Dave, Harry, Micky, Martin and I left. We got to the traffic lights and noticed the 'meat wagon' parked down the side of the Queens Head. 'This is it, we're gonna get done,' Dave said. I told them just to remain calm and act normally (as if they needed telling!). We crossed the road and passed the van. They looked out at us and we looked in at them. We kept walking – nothing happened. Andy couldn't believe it. The kids were surprised and seemed relieved.

'We were that close to them,' Harry excitedly said, holding his hands a couple of feet apart, 'and they didn't say a thing.' A discussion ensued as to why nothing had happened. Some said they weren't the usual police. My presence was suggested as another reason.

As we walked down Charles Street the kids were obviously apprehensive, turning round at the sound of each car. They were all keen to tell me of recent experiences with the police. Harry related how only on Thursday they were walking down Malling Road when the 'meat wagon' passed and all the police waved their helmets in the air as they passed, jeering at the kids. One policeman, recognising Andy, called out to him, 'Shoulders back, stomach in, left right, left right!' With this kind of behaviour – aren't the police inviting trouble?

Once into North Road we split into groups of twos and threes so as not to attract attention. We arrived at the Barge without further incident. I got the impression they were playing a well-worn path which had become second nature.

Andy was well 'boozed' by this time and the last to go in. I hung around outside to make sure he got in OK (rightly or wrongly I had adopted in this instance a rather protective rôle).

The Barge is a fairly rough place with a number of alcove seating arrangements down one side opposite the bar. Down the far end is a low stage with a disco area and a dance floor. By the side of the stage is an emergency exit. A fairly large area.

The Bs occupied an area to the right of the stage in the far corner. It wasn't long before they were fooling around dancing to the music. As far as I could make out they weren't drunk, but their manner suggested that quite a few drinks had already been tucked away. Harry came up to me. 'Hey, do you think I'm drunk?' 'No,' I answered, 'but you've had a few drinks.' The thing is, who decides when a person is drunk? How do the police decide objectively?

At 1.40 am the disco stopped and the bell rang for last orders. Most of the Bs were in the far corner. The place was fairly quiet after all the music. Then all of a sudden a fight broke out. Some bloke went over to the Bs and went for Eddie. This triggered it off. Everyone just piled in. Within seconds it was over and a number of people were hustled out through the emergency exit. Terry told me that Eddie had been cut. All of a sudden I felt insecure and very much out of my depth. Not really knowing what to do I followed Martin outside to look for Eddie. No one was outside, but after a few minutes Eddie, Andy and a couple of others came back. Eddie, stripped to the waist, covered in blood was clutching a piece of wood, determined to go back into the pub for revenge despite attempts to cool him off.

Fortunately (and I mean that), a panda car came

down the road. Seeing the car Eddie moved onto a piece of waste ground. The police, obviously suspicious, stopped. Eddie slipped round the corner and a policeman gave chase, but returned on his own. As soon as the police appeared on the scene I could sense that it wasn't so much rivalry between 'gangs' but everyone versus the police. No one saw or knew anything. . . .

After five minutes the bouncer wanted us out. Gary, Terry and I left and hung around for a few minutes looking cautiously for any police. Both Eddie and Gary were wild with anger. 'This is the second one cut.' I could sense very strongly their feelings of injustice and gross frustration at not being able to get revenge immediately. They very freely shared their feelings with me—I felt privileged. The three of us slowly walked home using the back streets to avoid the police.

All the way home their conversation expressed very strongly their feelings of powerlessness, the injustices that they'd received, and continual harassment by the police. Dave for example, during the evening at the Barge had said, 'Okay—I'm boozed, but not drunk. All I want to do now is go home peacefully and go to bed with no trouble.' It was all too clear that Dave was apprehensive about going home. He always had to take back roads and continuously ran the risk of being picked up.

These kids do not trust the police and the feeling of hatred and bitterness is very strong.

Terry left me with a disturbing last thought. 'One day, it might be soon, the police are going to stop and tell us to get in and we're going to say 'No' and face up to them and someone's going to get really hurt or possibly killed. It might be one of them or it might be one of us.'

This incident happened not long before the Bristol, Brixton and Toxteth anti-police riots in 1981. There was a climate present that was neither helpful to young people *or* police.

Another case came to my attention and I recorded it carefully at the time. Martin and Terry were genuinely concerned about being harassed. My reaction was to write the following letter with all the details being provided by the boys. The letter was then signed by the boys.

Dear Sir,
Official Complaint
I officially complain about wrongful arrest on Monday —th — 19—. We were sitting on a public bench at the corner of Smith Street and Wilson Road, at approximately 10.45 pm, on our own. Two officers in a Panda car approached us from behind and came round to us.

P.C. X approached Terry Brown, leaned over him face to face and said, 'You stink of beer and you are drunk.' Terry Brown said, 'What are you talking about, I've not had a drink!' The officer then grabbed his left wrist and top of same arm and pulled him up on his feet and led him to the police car. Terry Brown did not struggle. At the same time, P.C. Z approached Martin Smith and said, 'Come on, you as well—You're drunk.' The officer grabbed his left arm and pulled him to his feet.

In the car Martin Smith said, 'If you think we're drunk you must have a breathaliser in the car—use it on us—if it shows we've been drinking, arrest us, if it don't, let us go.' The officer (Z) said, 'We don't use breathalisers on drunks.' Martin Smith said, 'I'm getting in touch with A.10 – Oh, no CIB 2.' [A.10 was Police Complaints Investigation Dept., changed now to CIB 2.] The officer laughed and said, 'You are so drunk you can't say it!' Both asked to see the Chief Inspector, Mr White, and the officer said, 'He's home in bed – do you know his phone number?', mocking them, 'it's ex-directory.'

Entering the police station Terry Brown asked to see the Chief Inspector and Sergeant — grabbed his arm and pushed him aggressively against the charge seat and window. The officer said, as he pushed his face up to Terry Brown, 'Who are you talking to, slag? You are not in court in front of an audience.' Terry Brown said, 'I know what you want me to do,' meaning respond verbally or violently back at the officer. He did not respond.

Both young men asked permission to 1) make a phone call, 2) see a youth worker, 3) phone parents. The officer refused and mocked them. At no time were the arrested persons cautioned – even officially charged.

At no time had either young men had any alcohol during that day. Martin Smith was released at 2 am and Terry Brown was released at 3 am. Both given separate court dates, both were charged with being drunk.

This case actually went to court with a Police Complaints procedure hanging over it. The boys were found guilty at the local Magistrates Court, but later, having appealed to the Crown Court, the case was dismissed.

The next stage was interesting from a 'justice' viewpoint. The inspector in charge of complaints worked hard to get the boys to drop charges against his colleagues at the local station. If they had taken it farther:

– it would have gone to a police court, not a civil court

– the police would have had a Police Federation defence lawyer
– the boys would have had only a police inspector to represent them.

There seemed no justice possible even if they pressed ahead. Not wanting the hassle, the boys accepted the complaints inspector's 'recommended' method of dropping the complaint. I feel that justice was not done.

One evening we were called out by a distressed family because their eighteen-year-old son had been arrested on a drunk and disorderly charge and they couldn't gain access to him.

Two attempts from an agitated father had met with a cold response as the boy was supposed to have been, 'too drunk to be seen or released'. His father was also concerned, as his son suffered from epilepsy.

One of our workers, Alan, was called in as I was out. Using the Mayflower's name and his position as youth worker, Alan was eventually, at 1.30 in the morning, able to obtain his release. He noticed that the young man gave no appearance of being drunk. The boy told him that he had been standing outside a shop with a few of his friends. Because a police car and van were in the road he had walked away along an alley leading to another road. When he was twenty-five yards away from the main road he heard a bottle smash and his mates ran past him; he ran with them. He ran up the ramp leading to a tower block on his own. After a few minutes he came down the ramp and saw the police with his friend. He said he was about eight feet away from the bottom of the ramp when he hopped over onto the other path. Then one of the policemen grabbed him and said, 'You're nicked.' He asked what for, and the policeman said,

'For being drunk and disorderly and hurling bottles.'

Alan and the father took the boy straight to the hospital and used a procedure that we know can be relied on to prove the truth in these cases. Two blood samples were taken, placed in envelopes and signed by the doctor with the date and time. They were then taken to a laboratory which provides an independent service of analysing blood for alcohol content.

Eventually the case came to court. I heard the usual evidence of the police, which I've heard *so* often against our young people . . . 'I noticed, your worship, that his eyes were glazed, his speech slurred, he was unsteady on his feet, he was drunk.'

Normally the court believes the police evidence and there is a guilty verdict. In this case a witness from the laboratory presented the results. The level of alcohol in the blood sample was below the level of detection.

The case was dismissed. Justice had been done.

What do I mean by justice? And what is the Christian view on these matters?

It is interesting that 'justice' is mentioned twenty-six times in the Authorised Version of the Old Testament, but *not at all* in the New Testament. Many Christians are not aware of biblical teaching on justice because of this. The translators of the AV Bible translated the word 'justice' into 'judgement' in the New Testament. It is only since the modern translations, Todays English Version and the New International Version, have translated correctly, that Christians have been given a basis for a return to a balanced emphasis on justice.

Debby Kennett, resident and Team Assistant at Mayflower in 1985 came from a very live evangelical church in Cheam, Surrey. 'I was brought up to know all about God's *love*,' she said, 'but only when I came to the inner city did I learn of God's *justice*.'

In fact, the Bible stresses justice much more strongly than most Christians are aware. God makes it clear that he rejects our worship and prayer unless we concern ourselves with injustice and poverty. (See Isaiah 1:12-17 and Amos 5:21-24.)

The whole of Jesus' ministry commenced with his 'manifesto' in Luke 4:18-19:

'The Spirit of the Lord is upon me because he has chosen me to

- bring good news to the poor . . .
- proclaim liberty to the captives . . .
- bring recovery of sight to the blind . . .
- set free the oppressed . . .'

All this is justice in action, not just in New Testament days, but also *today*. It needs to be our manifesto also.

One day I had a letter from our local MP, Nigel Spearing, who had met a group of boys over a drink at the local Labour Party Social. He was concerned to hear their 'bitter complaints', and their confessions that, 'we are not angels, but the police are worse', and requested a meeting between senior police, the boys and myself. It seems the boys had confidence in Mayflower as a venue and Nigel Spearing himself set up the meeting and chaired it. He has always been supportive of the youth work at Mayflower and had a personal concern about the violence in the community.

The meeting consisted of three senior police officers, one probation officer, nine teenage young men, Roger Sainsbury (then warden of Mayflower), Nigel Spearing and myself. It was no light agenda. The nine boys present had received a total of forty-eight 'drunk' charges against them. Tony was the highest with nineteen charges!

It was not a slagging match, but a debate, and I am certain it did some good. Men in authority, in power, confronted young men with real feelings of injustice. Roger Sainsbury later gave a theological reflection which helped us all to think through the issues, not just concerning the police, but the whole youth work for justice. These are his conclusions:

Jesus and Justice

1. Bruce Reed in his book *Dynamics of Religion* says, 'If the Christian is worshipping his God with integrity we would expect his life to manifest the qualities of love, justice and righteousness because these are the characteristics he attributes to the divinity.' He adds later, 'Men cannot see the Kingdom. They can only see people overcoming injustice, maintaining righteousness, fostering creativity etc.'[2]

2. The club members at the meeting had three things in common:
   i. They all had criminal records. Some of their crimes they admitted but on other occasions they felt they had been treated unjustly and had lies told about them.
   ii. All of them over a long period had been under the sound of the gospel – thousands of words, logical arguments etc., had passed through their ears.
   iii. None of them had shown any real sign (despite many praying for them) of understanding the gospel of Christian commitment.

3. At the meeting the boys saw we were concerned for justice and truth. They also saw that, despite society's judgement of them, we accepted them as friends. The God whom we worship is a just God, His truth and His righteousness show themselves in graciously accepting as friends the publican and sinner. *His Kingdom is a Kingdom of justice, truth, righteousness and grace.*

4. Therefore at the meeting although nothing was said about Jesus, the Christian faith, the new life etc., I believe the gospel was being communicated in a powerful although non-verbal way. The club members saw something of the God we worship and they experienced something of the Kingdom Jesus is inviting them to enter.

Worship in spirit (from the heart) and in truth (directed towards a God who is true, just, righteous and gracious) must be a top priority for all our youth workers if we are to have the right attitudes in our work.

We must explore the injustices of the community in which our club members live, and stand by them as friends if we wish to communicate the gospel. This does not mean being 'soft on criminals' but it means applying justice and truth *both ways* – towards the authorities and towards our club members.

Biblical justice, however, is not just cold and clinical but includes in it the idea of 'ways of righting wrong' and 'setting right bad relationships'. Seeking justice in the community will therefore involve true reconciliation and better relationships in the community. Community involvement must therefore be a top priority for the youth work team.

Perhaps we also need to remember that we worship a God 'who believes in people' and we must reflect that in our attitudes to the young people of Canning Town.

Walking along the Newham Way the next day I saw Terry Brown – one of the club members who had been at the meeting. I asked him what he thought about the meeting and he replied, 'They didn't believe us.'

Many Christians may be disturbed by the way in which I

have spoken of the police. Church people generally have an image of the 'friendly British bobby', and have no experience of any abuse of police power. As a Christian, I don't want to seem to be 'police-bashing'. Each policeman and woman is, like all of us, created in the image of God. Each one has his or her divine characteristics and potential. Each one has also fallen and committed wrongs both personal and social, just like me!

It is also true that, individually and collectively, they have tremendous power together with government support in wielding it. I recognise that they have a difficult job to do, particularly in London, where one fifth of all UK crime is committed and only 17% of it is solved. They have to deal with some very difficult and violent people, and therefore need the support of the public.

'Much is required from the person to whom much is given; much more is required from the person to whom much more is given.' (Luke 12:48) This applies to the police, as to all in positions of authority. The police must keep the law of the land, and they must not break the law that they are employed to keep. All of us must work for justice in the making and changing of our laws and also in the keeping of them.

Half of those arrested in London are aged under twenty. Policing London costs £700 million, but the Inner London Youth Service costs £34 million. Is our society practising justice if we spend so little on the preventative, caring, educational aspects of youth work and so much on control and arrest?

'When the King is concerned with justice, the nation will be strong, but when he is only concerned with money, he will ruin his country.' (Proverbs 29:4)

Chapter 5

References

1. McKensie v. McKensie 1970.
2. Bruce Reed, *Dynamics of Religion*.

6: Deprivation

'Are you still taking the ugly pills?' I asked in my usual
jokey manner, but I did follow it up with a question that
was rather more serious and demanded more than a smile;
'You look sad tonight, Tina.' In the private conversation
that followed, and through the tears, she told me that she
had had an abortion just the day before – at five months
pregnant, and in hospital. She had actually 'delivered'
while she was alone in a private room. The nurses had made
comments like, 'It would have been a lovely baby – a
boy – if it had been allowed to live.'

Tina's parents are separated and she now lives uncom-
fortably with relatives. She says she prays – but that 'He'
doesn't do anything. She takes drugs and drinks regularly in
a number of pubs. She is beautiful. She is well-dressed. She
is fourteen.

We followed up this initial confidence with real caring
and support, but I need to ask questions – both as a
Christian and a youth worker.

What stops her conversion to freedom in Jesus? What is
stopping her development into a more able human being?

Kenny helped me to understand.

With the juke box beating and lots of the current popular
music and noise in club I approached Kenny as he stood
having a drink. He'd been sweating away playing football in
the gym again. ''Lright, Pip,' he said. He used my name.

81

It's always a good sign when kids use your name, it's meeting you. Kenny was nineteen and had been a regular for years, one of the 'Minis'. We chatted . . .

'How's your mum then, Ken?' I said.

He swore and mumbled something about not caring a damn.

'Do you not love your mum, Ken?' I went on.

'Nah.'

'What about your sister, Tracy, do you love her?'

'Nah,' was the curt answer and then the words came out like a torrent.

'Listen Pip, I don't love anybody, right. If I worried about paying my £250 fines, right . . . if I worried about being up in court next week, right . . . if I worried about being unemployed – *I'd crack up!* I love myself, nobody else, right!'

Some may take a hard line approach to this and think, 'That is why he is up before the court. This boy is a criminal, lazy, unemployed – totally selfish and self-centred. He needs changing from within.'

Yet there is another way of looking at Kenny, and I shared with him my thoughts about emotional deprivation. To cope with problems and issues in his life Kenny was pulling shutters down all around him. Survival meant numbing his own emotions. It was either that or go under. 'I'm like that, Pip – I admit that's what I do,' he said.

As a Christian there is nothing more exciting and fulfilling than to see and experience young people becoming Christians and seeing God do His special work inside them. It happened to me, why not Kenny?

Since his early teens, I and others have known Kenny and shared our lives with him. Jesus is always high on the agenda. Constantly, every day, conversations or exchanges take place in the youth work. And yet with so many kids the shutters are down, the numbing process shuts out God as well.

Exodus 6:9 speaks to me of a similar numbness. Moses was asked by God to speak to the people but when he did, 'they would not listen to him because their spirits had been broken by their cruel slavery'.

I have spent some time exploring the whole area of deprivation and I want to share my struggle of understanding with you here.

The Oxford Dictionary describes deprivation as being, 'Loss, being deprived, loss of desired thing'.

There are many aspects of deprivation, and there have been many books written on the different areas of deprivation. Some of these areas are: moral, sexual, linguistic, intellectual, environmental, physical, social, cognitive, spiritual and emotional deprivation.

First of all let's deal with what politicians call 'multiple deprivation'.

I am on the mailing list of the Inner City Directorate, which is part of the Department of the Environment, and they publish a great deal of statistical material on this issue. Basically they have chosen eight specific factors which are able to give an indication of the seriousness of deprivation in certain communities.

The factors chosen are: unemployment, overcrowded households, single parent households, households lacking exclusive use of basic amenities, pensioners living alone, population change, high mortality rate and households whose head was born in Pakistan or the New Commonwealth.

A word of caution on some of these, as none can be used in isolation to illustrate multiple deprivation. For instance the Isles of Scilly have a very high mortality rate, but presumably that is related to the high number of OAPs who retire there! Similarly Hove and Eastbourne have a very high number of OAPs living alone, which indicates that these are also popular areas for retirement. That doesn't make them deprived areas, however – it takes the other seven factors to be significant before a community registers in the 'top ten'. This is why we talk about 'multiple deprivation'.

Outside London it is Manchester, Leicester, Wolverhampton and Liverpool which head the seriously deprived list. Inside London the ten most deprived boroughs in order of seriousness are: Hackney, Newham, Tower Hamlets, Lambeth, Hammersmith, Haringey, Islington, Brent, Wandsworth, Southwark and Camden.

All this classification has resulted in extra government support to some areas of England. Some people don't like the phrase 'inner city'. It has become almost a catch phrase and is often misused. Many local people understandably don't like the word 'deprived' either. It sometimes hurts people who have lived long in a community and belong there in a most meaningful way. There is so much multicultural colour in Newham and I believe that is very good, although it also presents extra problems, as I shall illustrate shortly. The characters and personalities add the extra colour that makes the East End the place it is. But in London we can clearly see what has been described as the 'three ring city'.

One can imagine London as three concentric circles. The small central area represents the West End and the City, the traditional business, cultural, entertainment, tourist and shopping areas. Only 6,000 people actually live here.

The largest, outside circle represents the suburbs and this is a constantly expanding area. Here there are houses with gardens, a high rate of car ownership, open spaces. It has been described as 'the sugary outer edge of the doughnut'.[1]

The inner city is the middle ground between the central hive of activity and the suburban, largely commuting population. It is often an area of declining industry, inadequate schooling and housing, unemployment and racial conflict.

Newham and Canning Town are caught up in this mess which is made worse because of the decline of the docks. 'Jobs are disappearing fast, twice as fast as the population, and the population isn't hanging about.'[2] Due to the unattractiveness of the area there is much 'out-migration' of people, businesses, amenities etc. Special input is needed to halt this process; the London Docklands Development Corporation are attempting to do this as are other local bodies in various areas.

All this comes down to a personal level – how people live, what they own, what their opportunities are, what their feelings are. Deprivation affects *people*. The government tries to practise 'positive discrimination' in support of disadvantaged areas. *The Church doesn't.*

Words like 'deprivation', 'unemployment', 'delinquency', 'insecurity' are all negatives; they can only exist when opposed to certain opposite standards or expectations. It has been said that the study of deviance is ultimately the study of normality and because deviance is not a static state, neither therefore is normality. Perhaps there are things that once used to shock us, but now we are so used to them that they have become norms. The norms in our communities, our groups, even our families, are not necessarily normal in the next town, the next house. Normality is a shifting state, it is culturally defined, and before we can really look at deprivation we have to see first what is normal.

In my view, the male membership of the Mayflower

youth club see themselves as normal, yet usually 80% or more are deviant in that they have been arrested for offences or have a probation officer or a social worker.

We obviously attract youngsters who are 'street kids'. They are brought up on the street and that is their skill, craft and employment. We attract (whether we want to or not) a high percentage of teenage boys who carry knives, take drugs and are involved in planned violence (often football and racially motivated violence). They have other attributes, such as being unemployed, being from broken homes, handling stolen goods. They can chat normally when they are on their own, but are often aggressive, abusive, disruptive and irresponsibly dangerous when with a group of friends.

We also have teenagers attending Mayflower who are relaxed, pleasant, friendly and enjoy friendships and club facilities. They may have jobs or be unemployed. This category includes nearly all the girls, but only a small minority of boys. Those in the club who don't pursue criminal activity – that is, the minority – are seen, by the majority, to be abnormal, or deviant! Steve Rowgslie, writing on 'The Potential of I.T.' in *New Society* stated that, 'The minority who are too timid to share the joys of law-breaking are more likely than the delinquents to be maladjusted individuals . . .'[3]

I would say that the majority of non-delinquent males in the club are either loners or members of small peer groups. A member of a club or class being *too* friendly and helpful can be a bad sign. He may be seeking a relationship with an adult merely as compensation for lack of relationship with his peers. In many ways, helping a loner actually to join a peer group can be more helpful than allowing him a close relationship with a member of staff.

Regarding Christian conversion, it is often the case that if a loner makes a Christian commitment this can help to reinforce his or her aloneness and not help him or her in long term relationships. God brings people to Himself in varied ways, but we must be aware that a loner could be seeking our attention rather than that of the Creator Himself.

When I talk about emotional deprivation, I need therefore to look at what emotional normality or emotional wholeness is. I am so aware that emotions are part of our make-up, that they make us human beings. We are told that to develop 'normally', there is a hierarchy of needs.

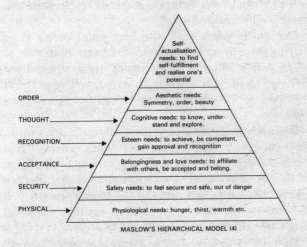

MASLOW'S HIERARCHICAL MODEL (4)

Physical needs are obviously most basic, and these are met for our young people (though even these are lacking for many teenagers in the Third World). Where our young people are lacking is in the areas of 'security' (social security is not enough), 'acceptance', 'recognition'. 'Self-actualisation' is just a dot on their horizons.

A more concise list, from the Director of the National

Children's Bureau, Mia Kellmer Pringle, is, 'love, security, new experiences, praise and recognition and responsibility'.[5] But human needs are not straightforward. Cows can manage with a field of grass and two milkings per day; plants need air, water, sunshine and soil for a normal life. The basic human needs are more complicated because we have psychological and sociological development as well as physical growth.

I have maintained for many years, in youth and community work, that 'our kind of kids don't *think*, they *feel*'. This is normality, it seems to me. It is not a 'put down'. When I was a teenager I responded to 'feelings' too, not to a self-actualised mind!

Our aim in youth work is to keep young people alive, helping them to establish identity and worth in relation to other people. When I say 'keeping them alive', I am referring to attempts to maintain their *capability to feel*. If there are no feelings then there is no life, there is mere existence.

If you see the gospel as something only spoken or written, you encounter an impenetrable block arising from emotional deprivation. You cannot get through! The Spirit of God is all powerful – I believe and *know* that. But 'an empty belly has no ears', says an old African proverb. Our kids are not actually in physical need, but their emotional needs are sufficient to deafen them.

However we mostly return to a more balanced or 'normal' frame of mind following a 'stretching' experience. But not necessarily: what if the emotional make-up is deprived in some way so as to prevent this return to stability?

John Bowley writes that 'even in so-called advanced countries there is a toleration for conditions of bad mental hygiene'.

There is, and rightly, great concern for the physically and

88

mentally handicapped in our society. But my own immediate personal concern is for the emotionally handicapped – the young adult the press refers to as a 'lout' or 'yob' or 'thug' or 'hooligan'. I believe that this young person is emotionally deprived, and needs not punishment but treatment, and instead of hostility and separation, needs to experience those aspects of love and security that have been lacking. It also hurts me deeply as a Christian to hear of young people being spoken of as 'louts' etc. Jesus loves these young people and we need to do so as well. It helps to understand when we love.

Jack Kahn, once psychiatrist to the London Borough of Newham, has said, 'Deprivation is only of value as a diagnosis when there is some awareness of lack of fulfilment of need, and where that awareness leads to some abnormal feeling or behaviour.'[6]

I could illustrate this with many cases of apparently senseless violence and deviant behaviour that I and my colleagues have witnessed at the Mayflower. It is my desire to understand the anti-social and violent symptoms of deprivation. But not just out of academic interest. Having had a tooth knocked out by a fourteen year old and a half brick thrown at me with accuracy . . . I am personally interested in alleviating it! Violence is a common reaction to deprivation but an alternative reaction to the situation is to become withdrawn. However, I agree with Christian lecturer and practitioner, Bob Holman, when he says, 'It is "more tolerable" for children to feel angry and hostile than to feel "loss or isolation".'[7]

Racism is a major problem in our area, and I believe that racism and racial violence is a cause of deprivation for the victims as well as a symptom of the deprivation of those participating in it.

Tony was a club member in the old days. Recently he stopped his car and jumped out as I was passing and we caught up on our news of the last three or four years. He told me that he still worked for the council as a jobbing painter and had been called several times to the home of an Asian family who had been repeatedly racially abused. Tony had been recalled so often to do a repaint on the front door which had been subjected to racist graffiti, that he himself had become a target for National Front supporters. They had daubed his car with swastikas and, following him home, they had broken his child's bedroom window. Tony's wife was now in hospital with severe eczema. They themselves had been rehoused and the case concerned made the national press, as the racialists became the first ever family to be evicted on grounds of causing racial harassment. It was bad enough for Tony and his wife, and he was only the painter! How much more pain and hurt did the Asian family who lived in that house have to suffer during that long period of racist abuse?

Mayflower itself has seen a good deal of organised racism. A number of our team of workers are black and Paul, my young professional colleague, has written of his feelings on entering the white-dominated club atmosphere:

'"Nigger!" shouts the white voice in the white crowd. I turn, hot, angry and shocked. I stare, my eyes fix themselves on the youth. The noise and activity of the club dissolves away. All I am aware of is myself and the other person. We are face to face.'

Three months later Paul was described in club as 'the one with the moustache'. From one of our highly racist young people this was a very positive comment and reflected, I am sure, the respect Paul had already gained.

Nothing makes me weep more than the racism I see on TV in South Africa – and feel in East London. It is our black brothers, sisters and kids who feel the hate and receive the abuse and yet it is a white problem. There are no black MPs, few opportunities for real power – all this creates a feeling of powerlessness that creates an *institutional racism*. I believe that until we become racially aware and begin to let go of the power that we hold as white people, we will never reach the wholeness that awaits us in Jesus.

Research has shown that the 'influences' of early childhood can affect people for many years, hindering their development towards maturity. 'It is possible to discriminate between potential delinquents and non-delinquents at the age of five or six.'[8]

John McVicar writes of his own aggression that was implanted into him at *pre-infant school* age. It doesn't end there either. 'Emotional deprivation can perpetuate the problem of violence in a chain of cause and effect from one generation to the next.'[9]

I once had a journalist from *Penthouse* referred to me because he was writing an article about youth gangs. He asked me why did kids turn out like this. I said, 'loss of adequate relationships'. He paused and said, 'you mean lack of love'. He spoke as though these were two different things, and yet love in action is best seen in relationships, in my view. The ultimate example of this is the love relationship offered to us by the Creator Himself. Love is a relationship of the most beautiful, intense kind. Some people have great difficulty forming relationships with anyone and there is a reason for this.

It is my view that emotional deprivation is caused by a loss of adequate relationships while other factors such as bad environment, education, and housing add to the problem but are not causes in themselves. It is often the lack of close family relationships that are at the root of violent behaviour.

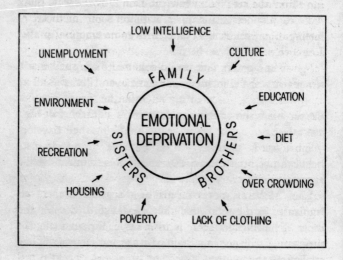

At the Mayflower we experience overtly demonstrated aggression and violence. 'Bashing' it is called. In the club the older boys bash the younger ones and they in turn bash the youngest. Try to picture a club with sixty or seventy teenagers engaged in normal activities – snooker, pool, juke box, coffee bar etc. Suddenly one group will jump on another and kick, punch, flail arms and fists. This is aggressive but it's not real violence. It is difficult to handle, however; it really disrupts the club and creates an environment that is not conducive to anything other than 'watch yer back', in case it's you who gets jumped on. Occasionally the atmosphere has changed from aggression to violence. In these cases it is usually a fringe member of a gang who is trying to impress by being violent and nasty.

All this has been complicated lately by smoke bombs. These implements of West Ham football 'supporters' have been tried out in club several times and add to the fun – from the kids' point of view. Don't, by the way, think that we just let this happen without some methods of intervention – we do intervene, with some emotion, prayer and energy.

It was in our old dark, multi-coloured disco shed that a seventeen-year-old member called me over. 'Pip' was all he said, but having attracted my attention he turned around, flashed his knife and began to destroy a fifteen-foot-high poster.

What was he saying?

All young people need an outlet for aggression. Some express this at work, some through sports like rugby or squash, some at rock concerts or discos. These are all legitimate in the sense that they are 'lawful'. But for the inner city youngster there is little outlet for aggression in their tarmac and concrete jungle with so few facilities. They are largely unemployed, bored and frustrated, devalued and de-skilled. Their chance for expressing themselves is more likely to be *watching* football and participating in football violence, or in the *disruption* of a disco or club activities, rather than through participation.

In my view, most kids behave in an anti-social manner without thinking. I am committed to creating opportunities to help young adults to express themselves. One boy said he had started to *think* before getting into fights. That is exciting!

It has been said that '95% of all crime is committed in built-up urban areas.'[10] Experiments show that a rat, when deprived of food and water will become as much as ten times more active than it would be when not deprived. When forced into crowded and stressful conditions, a proportion of rats become 'dominant' and 'criminal', characteristics they never assume in natural conditions.

Apply this to the urban teenager . . . we can see that hyperactivity can be the result of some kind of deprivation. Hyperactivity can be healthy, physically and socially, when channelled into something like sport.

But it can also be channelled into anti-social and disruptive acts such as vandalism and violence. Mia Kellmer Pringle wrote that 'violence and vandalism are probably linked to the most basic emotional needs and the extent to which these are met or remain unfulfilled'.[11]

If such symptoms are a response to needs not being met then it would seem that what is required for these deviant young people is not *retribution* but *restitution*. Our young people live in an environment where a certain level of crime, including violence and vandalism, is the norm. Children and young adults are set this example by strong visible adults in the community, often including parents and family. There is a lack of alternative adult models. We strive to provide these as Christians and youth workers in the community.

We are aware, in youth work, of the importance of providing primarily a *social* centre to aid the development of our members. For the teenager, the peer group is the main area of socialisation. In an urban environment, it is my observation that many parents have, to some extent, abandoned their children to their peer group.

In a 'normal' environment I believe that the peer group has immense development value, for, 'striking up relationships with one's peers, is, in its own right, a social skill . . .'[12] In East London, and other inner-city areas, the striking up of such relationships can be very much a negative one in that the social skills learned are often deviant. The more sophisticated crimes like burglary and warehouse-breaking are usually committed in smaller groups. However, much deviant activity happens in the context of gangs, as I have described. When the kids reach adolescence they are so insecure that they look to the gang as a source of fulfilment and achievement. They use it to assert themselves, in a collective way. Individually, they've been given the impression that they've got nothing going for them. Gangs meet some of the most basic needs as listed earlier: love and security; new experiences; praise and recognition, responsibility.

Dr Donald West, a famous British criminologist, quoting American studies, has described delinquent gangs as 'the inevitable outcome of the failure of the community to provide reasonable and constructive outlets for spirited and frustrated youth. Such gangs always flourish in the worst slums.'[13]

Billy of 'The Tramps' said once, 'Being together stops us getting depressed.' Belonging can be so important when life doesn't offer much else, when the young teenager longs to be accepted. 'We're all in the N.F. (National Front),' said Martin. 'Why?' 'Because they're really interested in us . . .' At the same time they don't actually think N.F. policies are good. They are just seeking acceptance, one of our basic human needs.

Sandra Warden writes that 'the more eager an individual is to become a member of a group, the more he will conform to its norms of behaviour'.[14] And S. Meyerson in *Adolescence and Breakdown* writes, 'Gang members can feel, at the height of gang violence, an almost orgasmic sense of belonging'.[15]

All that emotion and thrill is important to teenagers and rightly so. They need excitement and adventure and there is little hope of finding it in a society that lays on little other than unemployment and a boring environment to live in.

Back in 1978 I spoke on the Mayflower soundstrip about four of our members who were due in court for nicking £30,000 worth of stolen goods.

Now the thing is, these kids are handling this sort of cash. They don't work, they are professional criminals at a very early age. What can you offer teenagers like that? You can say; 'Be good!'; 'Settle down!'; 'Become respectable'; but – it's impossible! That sort of lifestyle is completely boring!

What have we got to offer in exchange for that lifestyle? I believe that the only lifestyle that can be better than that is a Christian lifestyle where it is challenging, where it's hard, where you can be laughed at, where it can be incredible but tough. And that's what I believe we need to do – offer to the kids the best.

My vision is that of young adults capturing the spirit of Christianity, *not* so as to become pathetic – following the norms of the institutionalised Church; but becoming dynamic, contemporary, plain-speaking, radical, politically, sexually, racially and spiritually aware contributors to community, society and world. Shalom!

Chapter 6

References

1. D. Wilcox and D. Richards, *London – The Heartless City* (Thames TV, 1977).
2. D. White, *Newham: An example of urban decline* (*New Society*, 1975).

3. Steve Rowgslie, *'The Potential of Intermediate Treatment' – Youth In Society* (*New Society* December 1975).
4. A. Maslow, *Motivation and Personality* (Harper and Row 1954).
5. K. T. Strongman, *The Psychology of Emotion* (Wiley and Sons 1973).
6. J. Kahn, *Human Growth* (Pergamon Press 1971).
7. Bob Holman, *Socially Deprived Families in Britain* (Bedford Sq. Press 1973).
8. M. Herbert, *Conduct Disorders of Children and Adolescents* (Wiley and Sons).
9. J. McVicar, *McVicar by Himself* (Arrow 1974/79).
10. A. Armstrong, *The Plague of Vandalism* (Local Council Review 1978).
11. Mia Kellmer Pringle, *The Roots of Violence and Vandalism* (NCB).
12. L. Button, *Development Group Work with Adolescents* 1976.
13. Dr Donald West, *The Young Offender* (Penguin 1967).
14. Sandra Warden, *The Left Outs* (Holt Reinhart and Winston 1968).
15. S. Meyerson, *Adolescence and Breakdown* (Allen and Unwin 1975).

7: Skills

I want you to listen to me as I communicate to you. I want you to listen as I explain how I understand things.

One day I was microwaving sausage rolls in the club coffee bar and Sandra, one of our workers, 'had a go at me'. She was leaving the Mayflower and she told me she was glad. 'Glad?' I said as I peeled the wrappers off the sausage rolls and tried to estimate how not to burn them. 'I'm sad you're leaving – and you're glad?' I had to press her for her reasons but she reluctantly shared them.

Two sausage rolls in an oven take the same time as twenty-two sausage rolls. But in a microwave it takes an extra four minutes for every extra one – and I puzzled to understand it! So I had eight minutes to listen to Sandra as she said, 'Pip, there is a black and white divide in the Mayflower.' She was speaking of the white workers and the black workers who staffed the day-time provision at the Centre. Sandra spoke as a black person. The whole issue of racism is that it is *felt* by black people and yet it is a *white* problem.

I am not picking up the issue of racism here, other than to say that I believe it is one of the biggest issues in society today. I'm picking up the issue of *listening* now.

With Sandra, I could have said, 'tell me what you think,' and then quickly said, 'Yes, but . . .' to every point she made. Instead I felt I had to *listen*. I listened with my eyes, my ears, my feelings. Not so as to interpret, not in order to think up answers and questions; I simply listened, asking questions only to clarify, to open her up more.

I had an unspoken commitment to listen. To think about what she said and evaluate it later. So often we evaluate while someone is speaking and that stops us listening.

We speak, apparently, at approximately 150 words per minute, while our 'thought speed' is 500-600 words per minute. As we all know from experience, our mind can become so active that we stop listening and go off on a thought of our own, only to come back seconds later having missed the point but politely nodding as if we know what the conversation is about! Our need to listen, to be listeners, is great. As Christians we don't follow Jesus in this respect. To listen we need to train our ears, mind and heart. It is an act of love. So many evangelical Christians are so keen to get their message over that they don't listen, unlike the Psalmist who knew the Lord's priority: 'You do not want sacrifices and offerings; you do not ask for animals burnt whole on the altar or for sacrifices to take away sins. Instead, you have given me ears to hear you.' (Psalm 40:6).

People who are 'print people' don't really understand how some can freeze at the sight of a page of print in front of them.

Literacy is a social skill that, if you have, you take for granted, and it most probably deprives you of sensitivity towards those who don't.

I myself couldn't handle a book until I was forty years old, and many others have this experience too. Yes, I could *read* by the age of eleven or so, but I only learned how to handle, use, dominate a book (instead of it dominating me) when I did my professional Youth Work training at Avery Hill College in London.

I always remember Ed at the Mayflower getting me to cash him a cheque during my early days. He conned me for £20. A learning experience for me! But I particularly remember what he said: 'I can't write real writing.' He was fourteen then. He knew how to handle stolen cheques, and several other 'skills' – but reading and writing were not two of them.

Jason had been involved in an attack on myself and another team member and was temporarily suspended from club. However, I was due to attend a court hearing with him the following week, and this went ahead as planned. 'This is er . . . this is er . . . this is the youth . . . er,' Jason stumbled out to his barrister on my arrival. He was pleased to see that I had come. He didn't say it but his face showed it.

Faced in court with so many officials and uniforms, the usual brashness and confidence shown by the teenagers drains away. Jason had his own mates as witnesses, to give evidence on his behalf, but he was found guilty of theft from a sweet shop in the West End. He had also broken into the kiosk and robbed it, but there was insufficient evidence for the burglary charge.

My rôle at hearings like this is to be a character witness after the verdict but before the sentencing. On this occasion Jason was only fined although he had been expecting a much tougher sentence.

Walking away from the court with Jason, I commented on how well his barrister had spoken on his behalf. I felt that she had been really sensitive and had worked hard for him. And Jason's reply was, 'You didn't do so bad yerself, Pip.' I had just exerted myself to the uttermost in explaining his level of criminality to the court, which had obviously affected the sentence, and yet 'you didn't do so bad' was his only recognition.

That is so typical of our young people. Jason was not

thanking me outright, but he was communicating in his own way and that meant a lot.

Denny sat down with me in the club and told me in a quiet and sensitive way that he had had £900 to spend just before Christmas, following the sale of stolen colour televisions. He knew he would get nicked eventually but his comment was, 'I've got a good wardrobe now. Something to fall back on.'

Is Denny socially inadequate? Approximately eight years later, having spent most of that time in prison, Denny sat in my office, and in the course of conversation on many issues he said, 'Listen, Pip, you'll never catch me in a council flat, living on a Giro. I'd rather spend four years in prison . . .'

Lots of children and young adults I know are only successful at one thing: *crime*.

The response of many Christians to all this is: 'Lock them up, that is what they deserve.' The hard line. I don't blame you if you think and talk that way. I used to. Everyone around me talked that way so it was 'normal' to take the hard line with the 'criminals', 'hooligans', 'thugs', 'louts' as the media calls them. I will repeat again that these kids are not thugs and louts, they are *people* – kids who I know. The Jesus of the Bible didn't look at and speak of human persons this way. Jesus touched the leper, forgave the sinner, ate with the swindler and thief, the publicans and the sinners (Matt. 9:11).

At fourteen Tommy would never be satisfied with one pound note in his pocket – it always had to be a roll of them. He never travelled by bus, always by taxi. He could nick any car on the road, whatever precautions were taken, said his probation officer. His favourite cars were BMWs, said the local policemen, 'because they can out-pace ours'. He has never had a job. Now in his very early twenties he owns property in Spain.

Some people think that someone like Tommy is unintelligent. This is *rubbish*. So many of our kids are not academic, not educated in society's terms, but are certainly not unintelligent. So many of our kids have not been able to cope with the education system, or it with them; their education has been 'street wise'.

At an early age too many kids learn how to TDA (Take and Drive Away) a car, break into the local dock warehouses, steal from shops and handle stolen goods. They graduate on to handling stolen cheques, and on to big burglaries. During recent summer months the boys have developed their skills. Resulting from experiences on football excursions into European countries, they have begun to purchase monthly rail cards – but not for holidays. In couples or small groups they go abroad to Switzerland, Denmark and so on, and steal expensive hi-fi equipment in quantity, before taking the train and ferry home.

As you listen to me, please don't make the interpretation that I condone this behaviour; I am just trying to make a point. 'Our Christian presence in the world is indispensable to evangelism, and so is the kind of dialogue whose purpose is to listen sensitively in order to understand.'[1] One point I could make is that I know about all this because I listen to the kids. They trust me, and that says something about confidentiality and getting alongside young people. Many people would say I should report them to the police. But that would end all my relationships and therefore my rôle and commitment towards their growth, development and wholeness in Jesus; end all possible chance of living in Canning Town, where to 'grass' is totally unacceptable behaviour.

The main point I wish to make is that all the 'skills'

developed by these young people are anti-social, against the society they live in. When it comes to the social skills that *we* have – and take for granted – they are, generally speaking, inadequate. Let me explain.

When you wish to make society work for you, you pick up a phone, speak to the right person, write a letter, approach the right people. So many people have these social skills and take them for granted so that they don't know what it feels like not to have them.

So many kids and young adults don't know where the handles, switches and buttons are. They don't know how to turn them. Knowing where the 'handles' are is important because it relates to power. Feeling inadequate is feeling powerless. 'Many young people,' says David Sheppard, 'have to make humiliating requests to officials'.[2] This applies very much to social skill and turning handles.

I have a friend who works in the local government housing department. When customers come to the hatch, it is normal, she says, to fob then off with: 'leave it with us'; 'you will get a letter'; 'the workman will call'; 'it's all going through' and so on. But if the customer says something like "I'm not satisfied" or "I want to speak to the Manager", then, she says, the whole office changes gear and the staff adopt a whole new approach. This customer has social skill – watch out! 'If we don't "produce", something will happen', she says.

Social power is taken so much for granted by the middle-class dominated Church; so much so that we oppress people. 'Mahatma Gandhi was asked what the greatest sadness in his life was, and he said, "the hard-heartedness of the educated" '.[3]

To say to deviant young people, 'Don't do it or we will imprison, punish, fine you' is to add to their oppression. I can identify with the Canadian rock singer Bruce Cockburn.

He described his visit to Nicaragua and his horror at seeing the deprivation, agony and hopelessness of the people in the refugee camps. The only medical supplies in that camp, he told the 1984 Greenbelt audience, were contained in the two suitcases he and a friend carried in. To add to all this, from out of the sky came the helicopter gunships, which brought terror into into the lives of these oppressed people. From that experience came his song 'Rocket Launcher':

Here comes the helicopter – second time today
Everybody scatters and hopes it goes away
How many kids they've murdered only God can say
If I had a Rocket Launcher – I'd make somebody pay[4]

He was, it seems to me, expressing the same anger that I feel when people want to punish and oppress the inner-city kids. Kids that have been made in God's likeness; kids for whom Jesus died. Bruce Cockburn was expressing the same anger that welled up in Jesus when he saw his Father's house being used by the powerful, to rip off the poor and powerless with their money-making rackets.

Jesus was angry then – but what does he think of our world today? The youth population has doubled since 1950 to 927 million, and yet they are offered little voice. Still less voice for young people who are inarticulate!

Never mind, young adults – we have a Lord of the 'underside' and one who will follow on from, 'Do not let anyone look down on you because you are young' (1 Tim. 4:12), with 'or unemployed, inarticulate, and powerless.'

William Temple wrote: 'My worth is what I am worth to God, and that is a marvellous great deal, for Christ died for me.'[5]

In a recent review of the Youth Service in England, it was

emphasised that 'the Youth Service's task is to provide social education'[6]. So many youth workers don't even understand what 'social education' is and most definitely don't see themselves as social educators. In recent years more local authority Youth Services have been handed over to the 'Parks and Gardens' dept, or the 'Leisure and Recreation' dept, and even the 'Museums' dept! A review of the Youth Service comes out, is presented to Parliament, and is virtually shelved with the result that the need for social education is not even being recognised.

Many youth workers, voluntary, part-time and professional, who are committed to social education, feel the kids' powerlessness themselves; they too feel in the gutters of society. They have 'gutter feelings'.

In the London Borough of Newham resources have been largely retained by a concerned council who support 'voluntary organisations' like Mayflower. But the pressure of rate-capping and the absence of real legislation for the Youth Service places us at real risk. Some local authorities have evaporated their Youth Service.

Christian youth workers are not much better off because they too often feel a separation from their church. The realisation that 'church' is 'bad news' and not 'Good News' for street kids is a hard one to take. 'Rate-capping' doesn't mean a thing to many Christians. My prayer is that the *Archbishop's Commission on Urban Priority Areas* (due to be published in December 1985) will make a big enough splash to send ripples through the whole of society, which I hope includes the Church!

One of the factors that keeps our young people 'underside' is unemployment. The massive unemployment problem in our own community needed and demanded a response. In the past we at Mayflower have sponsored various government

106

schemes to help alleviate the inactivity of unemployment. Before Y.O.P. there was J.C.P. and under that scheme we had a youth and community training scheme, a city farm in the Mayflower Garden and we also commenced our project to build a forty foot, twelve berth yacht out of concrete.

In the days when Y.T.S. was called Y.O.P. we sponsored several schemes that employed young people and adults and we continued building the concrete boat. Some ten years later this ferro-cement craft, named 'Cockney Spirit', is almost complete having also been the centre of a Y.T.S. and a C.P. (Community Project).

I won't go on to knock all these schemes because they *do* meet a need and are a better response from government than nothing. But it is not real work or adequate to meet the many needs of lots of our young people who can quickly become unemployable.

To receive 'the dole' helps survival but keeps the poor powerless. It helps to preserve dependency, and de-skills the young people concerned rather than increasing their social ability. It seems to me that to keep people in dependency is unjust and oppressive and therefore not Christian. It is *non-shalom*. Jesus came to release us for freedom for, 'there is more happiness in giving than in receiving' (Acts 20:35), and so many young adults have had no chance to give at all. William Temple is often quoted as someone who loved so much that he felt called upon to work for justice. He said 'The gravest and bitterest injury ... is the spiritual grievance of being allowed no opportunity of contributing to the general life and welfare of the community.'[7]

I have no easy answers but I'm certain that, like Jesus, we must not reject the leper, the disturbed, the prostitute – or the inner-city young adults.

Here is a letter I received from one of our teenagers in

prison. How did Ricky feel about his prospects? Can you catch his pain?

Hi, Pip

I thought I would write to you because I miss the Mayflower very much, but not to worry I should be out by Christmas.

I pray every night by my bed that Batman, Superman or God will come and forgive me and send me home . . .

I was thinking to myself and I thought I will be in prison all my life UNLESS I get a reasonable job but in our area – impossible. (Nelson has more chance of getting his arm back.)

I'm in a cell with a white kid and he keeps trying to crack me up, he's like a raving loonertick but he does have a radio, I think I can put up with him.

It's not bad here really but you can't call it good . . .

You know a few people in here but I'm not aloud to write any names. Thanks very much for the letter, I knew you would not forget me.
Ricky

Faced with the need around us, and realising the inadequacy of schemes, we had to ask, 'What else?' We sat down as a full-time youth work team a few years ago, Geoff, Ali, Doug, and myself, and decided we must set one of our number aside to head up a work for the unemployed. The local Youth Service were bound to 'evening provision' only, through tradition and lack of resources. There was no extra cash available but the youth work management agreed on a pilot scheme to be headed up by Doug McWilliams. Doug is a full-time colleague who felt particularly deeply for three unemployed young men at this time. Doug had picked up at first hand their hurt and their social handicap through their experience of unemployment. So 'Day Space' was born.

Day Space was to be for young adults between sixteen and twenty-five who had time to spare during the day. We didn't want it to be yet another 'drop-in' centre with predictable youth club activities during the day. The core of the whole scheme was to provide relevant social skills training. Don't imagine anything sophisticated! Kids would drift in and sit down with the daily papers and a spontaneous discussion would often pick up the current news topic. Following that, and when significant numbers arrived, the first hour was spent on the 'social skills' session as everyone sat around together. The range was wide but might include a video on a topic like sex education, racism, adolescence or drugs; a visiting M.P., careers officer, policeman; a debate on drugs, crime, unemployment etc; discussion and disclosure from the kids themselves about their own drug use, crime involvement etc. and their feelings about these activities. There was no 'curriculum', but, working under pressure, the Day Space workers prepared the most relevant, topical issue available. When an M.P. was arrested in a Soho gay club, the discussion was on attitudes to homosexuality, the police, authority figures, and the morals of M.P.s.

Doug once did a brain-storm on 'Deviance' with the kids. The results were as follows:

Deviant to Canning Town	*Normal to Canning Town*
Getting married	Football playing/watching
Illegal driving	Smoking 'weed' (marijuana)
Being a Christian or member of any sect	Smart clothes
	Unemployment
Molesting kids	Work
Football violence	'Pulling birds'

Deviant to Canning Town	Normal to Canning Town
Excessive drinking	Getting girls pregnant to get
Good education	a flat
Employment	Nicking
Being badly dressed	Being out late
Being gay	Being flash – 'macho'
Buying a house	Drinking
Talking to 'Old Bill'	Helping people
Grassing (telling tales)	Doing own thing
Regular routine	No faith in anything
Following the system,	Looking for trouble
school, job etc.	Hating police
Drug abuse (hard drugs)	Being generous
	Groups and gangs
	Winding up 'Old Bill'
	Fraud

This is *their* list without the deep debate to go with it!

Life here in Canning Town is not normal. Each community has its own sub-culture which is 'normal'. It is against that background that we are working to bring God's Kingdom to Canning Town.

I once did a brainstorm on 'How do we find a job?' The kids shouted out different ways of finding a job and we listed these on the chart: Jobcentres, local newspaper, 'on yer bike' (visiting local factories), careers officer, via relatives, phone calls, letters etc. Doing a handcount on who had used these was fascinating. Even the basic 'visit the Jobcentre' was so little used. Bones and Maurice confessed they visited three times a day, but others had been only once since leaving school. Years! They didn't know where the 'handles' were or how to use them. A good spin-off was that Gary, who hadn't worked since leaving school, was actually encouraged by this session. I guess he felt 'not the only wally'. Feeling inadequate together can actually be a strength. He chatted to Geoff, came in the day after, Doug made a phone call and set up an interview . . .

Just as there are *social skills* which help us to 'feel OK' in society, there are *political skills* which help us to change society. Many people I know don't like 'politics'. The word stinks for them. Many Christians don't see its relevance to them. Many middle-class people I know have no interest because they are comfortable with the status quo. Many working-class people have no interest either, because they think politics is for people with power and they feel powerless.

I stand and hold hands tightly with Christians around the world who *believe actively!* For example, the Post Green Community, who publish Grass Roots Magazine and say, 'Personal renewal for us involves opening our emotions to receive the pain of world affairs.'[8] The Christian faith isn't *just* a personal relationship with Jesus – it is personal, social and cosmic. Jesus love needs to stretch beyond 'my love for Jesus' to affect the community, borough, nation, Europe and the whole world.

But I don't advocate the American 'moral majority' approach. It seems to me they just concentrate on the anti-abortion issue which is 'for life – not death', but ignore other 'pro life' issues like inner-city deprivation, emotional handicap, bad housing, the gap between rich and the poor and the massive nuclear threat.

There is a great need for young people to become politically aware. The kids have strong views about things that affect their lives and I feel we could do much more to enhance this awareness.

As a Christian I obviously ask myself how my work relates

to the gospel, the Good News of new life in relationship with Jesus. At the Mayflower, my colleagues and myself are committed to evangelism, and all our social education inputs have a golden thread of explicitly Christian principle running all the way through. We have been accused of 'not being Christian enough', of 'only loving' the kids and being 'too professional'. But non-Christians reading this will no doubt criticise the overt religious directness. I can't win other than by being honest.

To be honest, then, I cannot divide the spiritual from the non-spiritual. If God is Maker and Creator of the world, and I believe He is, then He is concerned about the whole of it. The lot.

The Christian youth worker plays football with the teenagers in the gym for an hour and they come up to the coffee bar, drink Cokes together and talk about Jesus. Which bit is evangelism? The latter, most people say. Rubbish! You can't have one without the other. The whole life lived by the Christian is 'spiritual', including the sweat, the grazed shins and going to the toilet. We don't have Christians meals and non-Christian meals. We are not a Christian when we go to church and not when we go to bed. Most Christians believe this – and yet we need just as much to believe that as long as we are living Jesus' life, whether we are playing pool, pinball or having a deep conversation – we are sharing Jesus.

In fact, one exciting aspect of working with working-class youths is the total openness with 'God talk'. They may tell you exactly what *they* think as well, but Jesus *is* on the agenda. Jesus is on the agenda, and He will always be so in my life. His death isn't in vain as far as I'm concerned.

Chapter 7

References

1. Chris Sugden, *Radical Discipleship* (Marshalls 1981).
2. David Sheppard, *Bias to the Poor* (Hodder).
3. David Sheppard, Dimbleby Lecture 1984.
4. Bruce Cockburn, *Stealing Fire* L.P. (Golden Mountain Music Corp 1984).
5. William Temple, *Citizen and Churchman* (Eyre and Spottiswoode 1941).
6. Thompson, *Review of the Youth Service* (HMSO 1982).
7. F. A. Iremonger, *William Temple* (OUP 1948).
8. *Grassroots* (Sept. 1982).

8: Incarnational living

In the two months after I arrived at Mayflower, I threw all my training and experience with difficult youngsters of the past ten years out of the window. I was left with nothing but Jesus Himself: I had never talked to Him so much as I did during those months.

Seven and a half years later I was on the door during Senior Club, keeping an eye open for any possible trouble. Conversations were few that night so I began to doodle:

Pool, chips, tea, coffee, pinball, Jesus, pool, chips, tea, coffee, pinball, Jesus, pool, chips, tea, pinball, Jesus, pool, chips . . . that's how I feel.

Life seemed to be a never-ending circle of pool-table games and getting chips from the coffee bar. It seemed to be all that the kids were caught up in. Then I wrote:

Seven and a half years and no one wants to know Jesus.

That's how I was feeling that evening. Feeling low and discouraged; loving Jesus, but feeling very pathetic.

Why, I was asking myself, after seven and a half years of personal commitment and team work, are there so few individual Christians, and certainly no group of young Christian people, as a result of our work? Why do we fumble and

115

stumble over that great commission at the end of Matthew's Gospel, the 'making disciples of all nations . . .'?

A few days later I was reading in John 12:36, 37: 'After Jesus said this, he went off and hid himself from them. Even though he had performed all these miracles in their presence they did not believe in him . . .'

It hit me like a bomb. *Even Jesus had felt like me.* It gave me such help and encouragement to realise that Jesus was 'feeling' all this with me, and this lifted me up.

This chapter is mainly about 'pain'; about living it out in the flesh! It's hard to write because this pain isn't a concept. It's something felt deep down in my being. I have my *own* feelings to handle but also pressure from other people.

Often I'm told to give up the kids 'because they're too bad'. And humanly speaking there does seem little chance for the established criminal . . . but I know that Jesus died for the world, and that He never gives up on anyone. To feel battered, to go into club time after time and have to face up to conflict cannot be explained – only experienced. You have to prepare yourself spiritually and psychologically before club, to be ready for anything. The following helps to show why such preparation of the spirit is needed. I wrote this immediately following club in October 1984:

> . . . a night when there have been knives out and used as threats, large dangerous fireworks thrown indiscriminately and youth workers abused and threatened. It is impossible to place on paper what happened – and the atmosphere. Believe me it was horrible. The kids are so aggressive and explosive that even I, twenty years a full-time youth worker including ten years in Canning Town, cannot handle these hard tough teenagers.

That was what I was facing. That is what we, as a team faced regularly.

People expect a big set-up like Mayflower, with lots of youth provision and outspoken Christians, to produce certain results.

This sort of thing illustrates how it feels:

People say, 'No conversions?' 'No Christians?'
People say, 'You can't just love people!'
People say, 'Starting where they are at is not enough'
'What about SIN, conversions?'
'What about preaching the straight message of
SALVATION?'
'What about . . .'

Perhaps I should not work with kids I see in the gutters.
Perhaps if I aimed for those who would respond—
We would get more results. There are others
who are able to respond differently to our kids.

But who would handle the kids in the gutter?
Who else would take them in?
Who else would cater for their very basic needs?
They demand so much attention, their needs are so very
great . . .

I know eternal life is important! Vital!
Jesus came to make it possible! It cost!
All that is available to our kids and I know it is
important to be proclaimers of this Good News.

Perhaps I should leave here and take that Youth Leader
job—
In Sudbury-on-Thames . . .
Then I would have the satisfaction of an active fellowship—

Conversions and growth.
But what would happen – to the kids round here?
Signed Mother Teresa of Calcutta

It wasn't Mother Teresa who wrote this, of course – it was me! Written late one night after club, to make a point. It was written to say that there is less pressure on Mother Teresa to evangelise than there is on inner-city youth workers. There are fewer expectations from Mother Teresa than from rough council estate youth workers.

But don't think I am wiped out, burnt out, hopeless, faithless. No! I am just trying to paint a true picture – saying it how it is; how it feels. Gutter feelings.

I often quote David Sheppard's *Bias to the Poor*, when people ask me if I'm a pessimist: 'A television interviewer was talking to the Rector of Kirkby, who had been speaking of hope. " You are an optimist, then?" asked the interviewer. "I didn't say that," said the Rector. "I said that I am full of hope."'[6] Christian hope exists. I'm not so stupid as to think all 'bad' will be replaced by all 'good' – instantly! But . . . Jesus died that we might *all* have hope.

Very often, both at Mayflower and at the 'Y' Club in St Helens, I have been criticised by Christians for having non-Christian workers on the team. I was twenty-one years old before I became a Christian, after six years of nurture, discipling and training. As a Christian, I believe that God gives liberally to His creation, which includes all young people. There are so many qualities, gifts and skills among young people which they need to have the opportunity to discover and develop.

Mayflower, particularly well-known in evangelical Christian circles, often 'gets some stick' for unconventional methods of work. I agree we need it! We are not whole! We are not *shalom* before our God, or before the local Youth Service and the Department of Education and Science. I believe it is important that we own our imperfections and recognise our need for constructive criticism.

At Mayflower I started with a leadership team of fifteen 'residents', who were incomers into the Canning Town community, and myself as full-time youth worker. Indigenous leaders from the community were few and far between. Many locals were involved, but only a small number were involved in the actual hostilities of open youth work.

Over the ten years we built a team of seven full-time youth workers and thirty-five other part-time voluntary workers. Quite a number of these are ex-members of the club who have grown up into leadership.

Raf is a big, cuddly, black, cheerful, outspoken twenty-two-year-old full-time worker at Mayflower. He was once an active delinquent in trouble with the police and in the hands of the Social Services and Probation. The following are his feelings reflected on paper: '. . . never in my whole life did I think I would be able to do something I enjoyed . . . [meaning full-time work at Mayflower]. It has made me proud, made me more willing to try things that I would not have tried before.'

So many young people carry around with them a fatalism, an attitude that stifles hope and ambition. Bishop David Sheppard spoke of this in his Dimbleby Lecture. He spoke of 'A poverty that imprisons the spirit.'[1] That is not Good News. As a Christian youth worker I see the need to bring the Good News of God's Kingdom to bear on that poverty. Not a challenge, threatening and oppressing, but affirmation, building up and *true salvation*. Salvation meaning not only new spiritual life in Jesus, but also true freedom, opening up like a flower to the sun. You know, for most of my Christian life I understood salvation to mean the act of being 'personally' saved by Jesus, i.e. being 'born again' by His Spirit, which of course it does mean. It happened to me and I in turn actively communicate that Good News to people all around me. But I have lived in ignorance for so long not knowing that salvation is *also* about the wholeness journey. I have learned that that word 'salvation' came first from the Old Testament (Exodus 14:30) when the Israelites fled from Egypt and experienced liberation, freedom, release – in fact an opening up to a full life. That is what salvation means to me now.

Raf has experienced that also and he has become participant in his own destiny. He has joined the 'wholeness road'. He was experiencing the benefits of 'salvation' without, at that time, being willing verbally to express Jesus as Lord and Saviour.

Alan Griffiths was another long term club member who used to be a member of the 'Mini Snipers'. In 1984 he came into employment with us following a term in prison. It was his *first job ever* and he was twenty-two years old. He admits that he used to think of the leaders as totally alien to him, just people he could enjoy 'winding up'. Now he can relate to us, to the work, and he is thankful for useful employment.

This is an example of participation. Bringing young people into leadership. Making people whole and introducing them to God's Kingdom. As I write, Alan Griffiths doesn't confess to being a disciple of Jesus. He has experienced the fruits of God's Kingdom, but has not entered it himself by new birth. It is just as it was for the nine lepers who were healed and went away. They benefited from the 'salvation of healing' without entering themselves into a believing community. But God has not finished with them yet – or you or me indeed!

Back in January 1981 I wrote, 'Finding new workers is a

problem. We can get people from outside the community, but it seems to me that more than anything else we need to "grow our own", from among the local kids and young adults.'

Raf, Al and others can't be called 'a bunch of weirdos' who come from 'swede villages and farms'. Perhaps society writes them off as anti-social, deviant, uneducated; but in Canning Town they have credibility. They are streetwise, East-End wise and indigenous leaders. When Jesus became flesh in our world He came as a Jewish Palestinian male. He didn't come among us cultureless and sexless. He came and made common ground with the people of the day and contextualised His lifestyle.

We, as leaders, often keep all decisions so close to our chests that we cultivate powerlessness in those we lead and therefore enforce the continuance of childhood among grown persons. Leadership can be oppressive and not about release and freedom.

It's in 'letting go' that we can receive as well as 'it is in giving that we receive'. (St Francis of Assisi)

We still suffer from the same problems at Mayflower. The incomers are Christians and the Canning Town kids are not. Christianity is seen as a middle-class articulate thing. It's something *they* have, not relevant to *us*. I really do believe that, in harsh inner-city areas, short term contact and sharing of faith is largely ineffective. Some people will say this devalues God's power and the work of the Holy Spirit. Not so. Jesus Himself came and lived for thirty years among a particular community before starting an active ministry for three years. He was no incomer. Roy Trevivian, an ex-Mayflower chaplain, said on the Mayflower filmstrip:

The Mayflower's main task, it seems to me, is to be a beacon of caring allied to hope. The Mayflower Family

121

Centre must be seen as a place where there are people who care, where we're willing to start with the problem they've got, but lead them on to a relationship with Jesus . . . that is going to be a long, painstaking, very demanding job. No one should come and work at the Mayflower if they expect success overnight. The idea of a ten-day mission campaign that is going to convert Canning Town overnight is a load of utter rubbish.

It's the slow, persistent, unbreakable loving care that goes on day after day after day, that eventually is going to win the trust of these people. And in my experience moments do come, not many, but do come, when because people trust that you care, you have the chance then to say 'and I know someone who cares for you even more . . . and that's Jesus Himself'.

Resulting from this realisation we changed our criteria at Mayflower for residents who came and lived in the hostel with us. Two years became the minimum.

In the early days we were more confident that we knew how to bring the reality of God's love to the reality of life in Canning Town. There was, at that time, a clear strategy. In my reports over the first few years I repeatedly referred to how 'settled' the club had become and how relationships had deepened. How people had made Christian commitments. I recorded about what happened to Joey . . .

Joey is famous for his enthusiasm for West Ham football club. He has 'West Ham' tattooed on his chest, 'F.A. Cup' on his stomach.

Joey had been referred to us by the Probation Service and he became a voluntary youth leader in club. He was a real good worker particularly involved with the football side of things.

He left London a few months later due to personal problems, but one Saturday morning I bumped into him. He talked to me for over an hour about his problems, then asked me how he could become a Christian. Sometime later that morning he prayed out loud, weeping as he asked Jesus to come into his life and to change him.

But we hardly saw him after that.

I also recorded my delight in having 300 come in to church for the showing of the film *The Cross and The Switchblade* starring Pat Boone and Nicky Estrada. And how sixteen young people had been 'converted' after the showing of the film. But again we saw little response from those sixteen young people, even though we prayed and worked hard at bringing them into Christian growth experiences. The reports returned time and time again to trouble in club and disillusionment.

A quotation from David Sheppard's *Built as a City* was often used during this time, and regularly ever since: 'The greatest quality of a youth worker is an enormous capacity for disappointment.'[2] We were getting conversions but also disappointments. The answer wasn't 'conversions' but 'making disciples' (Matt. 28:19). We knew it – but we had to start to operate long-term Christian youth work to bring Shalom up front in people's lives.

Our strategy was a long one which included, as one of its main aims, team building with a special emphasis on indigenous leadership. Staff changes began. Our first team assistant was appointed in May 1976 after fifteen months full-time alone. Dick Betterton joined me in this one year training post and immediately brought a bond of close fellowship to us. I remember clearly when he was arrested with a minibus load of kids on the M1. A Manchester

United supporter had been stabbed by one of our kids and the police put every one of them inside, including Dick, the youth worker. It was a very serious incident but, as with most things, good came from it. Dick became really accepted because he had stood among them, as one of them, in their time of need. The kids still talk about that incident, nine years later.

Then in September 1976 I gained my first full-time permanent colleague. Kris Traer. She was twenty-three, professionally-trained and an experienced youth worker, and she was a blessing to all the team. The real blessing came not from her training and experience, but from her enthusiastic love for Jesus and its expression among and for the kids. I always remember saying to Kris when she left and got married to Dick, that among all the trials and stress we experienced together, she never lost that beautiful glow of enthusiasm called faith.

I would never say that the youth work at Mayflower was successful, only that it survived. Survived against all odds in demonstrating the Kingdom of God in Canning Town.

One breakthrough in leadership and team work terms came when I broke. My previously established leadership method of being in charge, a charismatic up-front decision-making leader was broken. I remember the evening; there was a gang at the front door armed with their axes and hammers and I couldn't face them like I usually did. I was up-front in everything, but not that night; I had to leave it to other team workers. At the same time the Rifle Range had broken up in disruption and another group of kids were running over the Mayflower roof shooting air guns. That was the night I went from 'topside leadership' to 'the underside'. To understand this means understanding vulnerability. Ideally we need to *choose* to be vulnerable, like Jesus who, even though He was God, chose to come among us in human likeness, from a position not of power but of weakness. 'My power is strongest when you are weak,' our Lord says (2 Cor. 12:8). I didn't choose this way, but was forced into it by violence. Now I believe this way is right and it has changed the way I work.

Instead of me listening to the kids and the youth workers' opinions and then making the decisions, i.e. *dependency* on leader, decisions became team decisions, i.e. *inter-dependency*. From then on I remained senior youth worker, but I saw my leadership as function and not status. I still led the team and chaired the meetings but I tried to cultivate cohesiveness or, in Christian terms, true *Koinonia*.

I believe that Jesus, the greatest leader we can model ourselves upon, practised an inter-dependency leadership method. He came as a suffering servant (Isaiah 53:3), not as a king on a white horse with polished armour. He came not as a king with powerful armies, but as the Prince of Peace, or *Shalom*. *Shalom* means peace, and comes from a verb meaning 'to bring to completeness', 'to make whole'. Jim Punton, FYT training officer, says of this word *Shalom* that 'it speaks of a totally integrated life with health of body, heart and mind, attuned to nature, open to others, in joy with God. It speaks of sharing, mutuality and love; of justice, freedom, interdependence, reciprocity.'[3] 'For in him (Jesus) the whole fullness of God dwells bodily.' (Col. 2:9).

My brokenness at that time, I believe, made me identify more and more with Jesus. I searched and adopted *His* youth work style. I sought then and remain actively pursuing, the leadership standard of Jesus, aiming at 'reaching the very height of Christ's stature.' (Eph. 4:13).

In one of my favourite books *I'm OK – You're OK*, there is a list of three reasons why people change:

1. Slow despair, boredom.
2. They hurt sufficiently.
3. The sudden discovery that they can.[4]

I HURT SUFFICIENTLY.
I hurt so much that I changed.
That new emphasis reminds me of this leadership course:

A short course in leadership:
The six most important words—
'I admit I made a mistake.'

The five most important words—
'I am proud of you.'

The four most important words—
'What is your opinion?'

The three most important words—
'If you please.'

The two most important words—
'Thank you.'

The one most important word—
'We'

And the *least* most important word—
'I'[5]

Let's go into club again . . .

Hanging around were about twenty 'boys' of between nineteen and twenty-two. The main preoccupation was getting
cups of tea from the coffee bar. It was well past 10 p.m. and
the Late Club was even more busy and noisy than usual. I
forced myself to sit down, though when you're tense it's easier
to stand or walk around.

Eddie was sitting on the Juke Box about thirty feet away. I

dived in. 'Well, Eddie,' I said. 'When are you going to become a Christian?' 'What do you mean, "a Christian"?' he asked. 'What exactly *is* a Christian?'. (That question excites me!) And he even walked over and sat down opposite me.

Eddie and I then sat talking seriously about Jesus, about being secure, about self-worth, love, sex, in an open question and answer debate. I shared Eddie's chips. And some more boys joined us.

I had known Eddie for seven and a half years, years consisting mainly of confrontation with him and court appearances on his behalf. He has even been before the court for attacking a youth worker in the past. And in my case I had had years of soaking in his verbal abuse and experiencing his withdrawal if ever more than one sentence was spoken. This chat was the first *real* conversation I had had with him in over seven years of youth work. Don't get me wrong; I have often tried. It seems to me that prior to this he had simply been too insecure to chat, too much influenced by peer pressure. Not until now, at twenty, was he secure enough to relax and relate with me. Now I would love to see Eddie become a Christian. He didn't become one when this encounter took place. He still isn't a Christian. We have eagerly pursued his growth for years and have seen him develop in social terms. (Not *too* much, though – he is still active in serious crime.) So what does being a Christian mean in inner-city youth work?

The Incarnation is about God becoming a physical body – *in the flesh*. 'The Word became a human being and . . . lived among us.' (John 1:14). Incarnation also means, to me, the living presence of Jesus *inside me*. The verse from the Living Bible which I often use as a simple definition of a Christian is: 'If anyone hasn't got the Spirit of Christ living in him, he isn't a Christian at all.'

Since I first became a Christian, I can honestly say I've *never* felt, or believed, that Jesus has left me. Even with pain and pressure which has made me often say, 'Why, Lord?' or 'I don't understand' Jesus has remained the primary motivater in my life.

Incarnation in the youth club, among young people, is presence without oppression. That is what we strive to live out and the result, we have come to realise, is not the message. The medium is the message. The individual and team life as youth workers must demonstrate Jesus' reign within us. What we do, must match what we say. We are not proclaiming a concept, 'four gospel laws' or whatever, but a Kingdom where God reigns and others are welcome – very welcome indeed! 'The Kingdom of God is justice, *shalom* and joy in the Spirit' (Rom. 14:17, N.I.V.).

I do, however, feel oppression from some evangelical Christians. That is the reason I wrote the Mother Teresa poem above. I need to keep reminding myself that the depth of relationship isn't limited to the quality of conversations. That the depth of Spirit isn't limited by the quantity of conversions. That the depth of God's life-changing work isn't limited by my desire or what I see as results. That our work for Jesus isn't done for results but for love and by love and in love.

'I may be able to speak the language of men and even angels and get results but if I have no love, my speech and youth work is no more than a noisy bell . . . I may have the gift of inspired preaching; I may have all knowledge and understand all secrets, I may have all power to convert young people, I may have all faith to move mountains – but if I have no love, I am nothing.' (My paraphrase of 1 Cor. 13:1, 2.)

Coming here and living in the flesh cost pain, tears, insults, abuse, judgement, spit, burn-out, disappointment – and eventual lashing and crucifixion. Yes, the cost of bringing the Good News to this cosmos *cost*. It cost the most anyone can give. Painful death and all that led up to it. God so loved the cosmos that He gave His Son.

What has it cost Joan, Joy, Ann and myself to be a Christian family in the flesh in the inner city? For a start we came from a working-class background, and where you *come from* is very significant. The industrial north is a tough territory but coming to Canning Town hit us very hard. Many people from a middle-class background are hit even harder. Others – but so many others don't even contemplate moving from their own social strata into another. I have my own paraphrased Bible verses written in my diary: 'He judges in favour of the oppressed and gives food to the hungry . . . Sell all you have and give to the poor . . . Ha, ha, ha, I was only joking, stay as you are – I really didn't mean to disturb you . . .' (Ps. 146:7-8; Luke 18:22).

Joy, now eighteen and a fashion student, has gone through the local education system. Ann is currently at comprehensive school in what is, according to the statistics, the worst education authority in the country. I want to write personally about my own family, but I must make the point that *all local kids* go through the local education system. Kids of our friends. Friends of our kids. Kids of Mayflower church members. These incredible Canning Town East Enders are used to life here and generally speaking adjust to it. But even when acclimatised to inner-city life local families feel the pain. We all do unless we lock ourselves away indoors and never come out. A serious threat of violence against a member of your family; your son arrested for theft; father slashed with a glass in a pub; son charged with murder; nervous break-down; pregnant daughter; racist attack. All these are not just experiences of East End criminalised families, but experiences of Mayflower *church members*.

People with families will understand how busy family life can be. In comes Ann with homework or friends – sometimes both! Shopping, phone, meals, visitors, pick up Joy from college, a knock at the door, a shout, 'It's some boy for you, Pip' . . . Can I never go to the toilet?

Often as a married couple, Joan and I need to catch up on each other. All the activity above often means we 'see' each other but do not share, talk out, catch up and basically communicate. Before club is no good! During the day before going into club Joan may wish to chat about something, but I'm no good. I'm preoccupied emotionally preparing for conflict, emotional intensity and possibly violence. I can't concentrate or relax before going into club. I eat too much or not enough, am touchy, tense and often have acid in my stomach. At the worst times there is little sleep at night – only sweating.

I have come to understand something of our A.N.S. (Autonomic Nervous System) which operates when the brain regulates to our external and internal environment. Before club nights my constant 'battle stations' create indigestion. A psychologist described it as a response to fear:

Suppose, for example, that something frightens a person. In such a time of stress, the sympathetic system predominates. As adrenalin is released into the system, many changes in body function occur: the pupils of the eyes dilate, the eyelids lift, the eyeballs protrude, the heart rate increases and blood pressure is elevated; the volume of blood in internal organs decreases and more blood is pumped to the extremities and muscles; blood sugar is increased, digestion ceases, and the spleen pours out more blood cells to carry oxygen.[7]

Indigestion tablets have been 'tools of the trade' for me for years. Other workers suffer differently. A number suffer from skin disorders, or a far too regular common cold. Red rashes to the face, blains to the eyes, cold sores to the mouth, weight loss! One of my colleagues was a regular blood donor before and after her time at Mayflower. Over a three year duration of inner-city youth work her blood became unacceptable!

To add to the regular pressures, there have been the irregular ones. I can remember returning from an Old Bailey court appearance with club boys, to find Joan so much under pressure that we just had to get in the car and drive and drive, to escape the intensity of life. Have you ever felt so much pressure that you feel as though your head might explode? Only getting away can give you some sort of emotional space. But we have to return eventually. Return to . . . the kids' bedroom windows getting broken so often we had to have plastic glass put in them. And stress hit all the family when the Mayflower switchboard constantly rang through to our house, night and day. We've had people coming to the door with nervous breakdowns and sometimes we were feeling in a worse state ourselves.

The shortage of finance to afford a trip out, or a holiday, added to the pressure. I remember a rainy holiday with a borrowed caravan and a total budget of £2.50 a day. We returned the worse for wear.

At an FYT youth workers' event in 1983 a participant wrote a Christian song that echoed many youth workers' experiences – most certainly ours.

> Lord of our city, we bring you its pain
> The muggings, the dole queues,
> The lift's bust again.
> The fear of each stranger –
> And nowhere to play.
> The waiting for buses at the start of the day.

Lord of our homeless, we bring you their cry
The waiting on promises—pie in the sky.
The red tape and questions and
Sent on their way
The sense of frustration at the noon of the day.

Lord of all races, all colours of skin,
Please make us fight racism,
Let us begin
To see how our prejudice colours the way
We treat friends and neighbours
At the end of the day.

Lord of our whole lives, we bring them to you
We're powerless, defeated till
You make us new,
Then powered by Your Spirit, we
Go on once more
With news of Your wholeness
Good News for the poor.[8]

That is some of the pain when living an incarnational life-style. But it's not all pain. There is action, involvement, joy, laughter—especially when working the Good news out in the context of team work. One whole aspect of incarnational living is that it is *not* meant to be lived in isolation. David Sheppard says that, 'the greatest resource the church has to offer is its army of lay people . . .'[6] One thing I don't want to do is to set myself up as a 'Youth Work Superman' or guru figure! Nor do I want to make out that Canning Town is worse than everywhere else—there are many similar environments in this country. I've led the team at Mayflower but have very much tried to do this 'from below', 'as one of', 'from among'.

'Christian leadership,' says Max Warren, 'has nothing to

do with self-assertion, but everything to do with encouraging other people to assert themselves'[9]

We have an incredible team at Mayflower with everyone having so much to offer. But each worker has a unique and individual style with the kids. There is a wide range of personalities and approaches between us. There is no 'right way'. But we train ourselves to extend our individual contact-making skills. Some need to be more chatty, some more physical, and we try to extend our repertoire of relationship-building methods. Not that we can ever sit back when in club; often the situation and atmosphere changes rapidly and this demands the utmost from us all as we handle conflict and tension.

Everyone with so much to offer alongside our fears, feelings, and failings. Each of us has a style:

Dave	either launches into games at the pool table, moves around rapidly, hugs the girls, jokes with the boys. Lots of humour and gentle extrovertness.
Debbie	also moves around but uses all sorts of instant 'specials' (paper or table games) to make contact which often ends up in a long deep chat with someone in need.
Geoff	moves around easily in the gym making physical contact with a large hyperactive disruptive group of boys through games for football – blood, sweat and tears! This too ends up with chats leaning against the coffee bar with a glass of milk.
Margaret	too moves around but often chatting to kids about school and the family networks she knows so much about. Her style is different because she knows their sisters and brothers via her own three children.
Patrick	jokes about making good contact in the showers (!)

	but other than his football contact, he tends to dive right in by asking personal questions.
Mark	uses the club keys to make contact. He is approached to fix the pool-table and then often spends much of his time with one or two members.
Joy	is quieter. She moves around and befriends both sexes gently. Her girls' group often come in to engage in long chats which in turn spin off into relationships with boys.
Liz	too is a quiet worker. She often stays close to one group of girls all evening as they attach themselves to the pool tables.
Pat	has all the local gossip and is fashion conscious. The boys joke with her and she beams and laughs readily with them which can lead to intimate conversations. She touches when she talks.
Johnny	is more static in the weight-training room. The chat is wide-ranging but comes from a basic interest in one activity.
Pete	too is static as he mans the door. He knows everyone's name and who is in club or not. He loves a wrestle with the boys.
Joyce	is approached as she mans the coffee bar, 'Hello mum, can I have ...' She provides a non-threatening security.
Pip	moves around the club greeting people with punches or kicks! One-line jokes, hugging girls, getting involved in games – often leading to deep, sitting-down conversations about court cases, family problems etc.

None of us individually has the whole repertoire. Only Jesus, it seems to me, has the wholeness that we aim for:

'For the full content of divine nature lives in Christ, in his humanity, and you have been given full life in union with him . . .' (Col. 2:9, 10). For some years I have kept a diary on 'the repertoire of Jesus'. As I discover His ways from the 'manual', and experience him in others, I note *His* style, *His* leadership.

It's been said that, 'although potential leaders are born, effective leaders are made'.[10] Jesus said to an ordinary but mixed bunch of men, 'Come with me and I will teach you to catch men.' (Matt. 4:19). I have spoken of 'Get Lost' theology. The Incarnation Way is a 'Get Out' theology. In the words of Jesus, 'As the Father sent me, so I send you.' (John 20:21).

We are called to express Jesus in our lives – that is what 'incarnation' means – He lives through us, in our bodies, and in our gestures, postures – in all our communication. We also need to learn from Jesus to read and use other people's communication.

Aggro had been 'barred' for a week for disrupting club with a group of others. Spitting all over the pin-table, throwing litter bins, kicking the juke-box etc. That's a brief description. There is much more feeling in it than a few words can express.

The conflict had built up between this group and the youth team. They eventually 'steamed' the door and, although suspended they were *in* club. Sometimes in youth work a sensitive confrontation with a member will result in something positive. Anyway, on this occasion, I was mad and he was 'humpy' and aggressive.

I threatened him with a phone-call to his family – but backed down for fear of breaking the relationship we had and he stayed in club knowing he had stretched the boundary beyond the acceptable behaviour.

During the next week he was fascinating. He was regretful of his violence, abuse and aggressive attitude, *but didn't say it*.

One evening I was sat by the snooker table deliberately quiet and not starting interactions with him or his mates and this is what Aggro did:

1. He walked past me twice and came out with a friendly comment to his mates about me.
2. Minutes later, he came and sat by the side of me, two chairs distance away from me.
3. He next walked around the snooker table twice and came and sat at my shoulder in the *next* chair. Nudged me with his shoulder and commented about the game.
4. He then walked twice around the snooker table and came and stood at my side, saying something irrelevent, he brushed my hair straight on my forehead before walking around the table again.

He was saying so much with his body language.

Later on that evening I responded positively to *his* communication by punching him twice in the ribs and smiling. From then on we picked up our relationship where we had left off.

If you visit the Mayflower Club on a Senior night you will be asked not to stand still, back against the wall with arms folded and looking around constantly. If it's not possible for you to roam around making friendly contact with groups of kids, you will be asked to, at least, sit down with a cup of coffee or a Christian comic. Your body language can do so much to influence the club atmosphere in a bad way.

Almost every time there are visitors they are uncomfortable in the kids' atmosphere. It's OK if they can engage in conversation. Articulate people lean to the known for comfort. Left alone they invariably stand up, arms folded, lean against a wall and look around. Our kids don't do this and they feel it when others do.

Standing is an aggressive posture compared with a seated or lower position. People often bow or curtsey to royalty ('Highness' indicates superiority). When you are nervous and apprehensive it is difficult to sit down and relax. It's easier to stand in the 'be prepared' position. Experienced youth workers still feel this apprehension but force themselves to sit down in a hostile environment, otherwise it increases the tension.

Arms folded is the traditional defensive posture for all people whether they are business people around a boardroom table or visitors to Mayflower. It is most often done by strangers in groups whether in cocktail parties, pubs or clubs. Lots of people claim they only do it to feel comfortable, to change body posture, or because they do not know what to do with their hands. That is the point – because your attitude to the group or person you are with is negative, you fold your arms for comfort. Christians from middle-class suburbs often visit Mayflower on Sunday evenings. After church, mixing with their peers, they speak with arm gestures. But when they come into club up come the arms to folded position.

In my approved school days you learned quickly never to sit on an inside edge of a table, but always on the outer edge with your back to the wall. You can then see everyone. Even now, twenty years later, I go into the Wimpy Bar for a coffee with Joan and sit with my back to the wall. So it is with our visitors. It's safer to be 'back to the wall'.

Look into people's eyes when they are scared and the adrenalin pumps, then they close. 'He looked daggers at me' or 'her eyes seemed to pin me to the wall' are both common observations of eyes that appear to be hostile. Then there are eyes that swivel around – 'shifty eyes'. Nothing is worse, eye-contact wise, than when someone keeps giving you sideways glances. But eye contact can also be very positive – communicating warmth, warning, sharing a joke. We need to learn to use it positively – to stop our eyes from being too 'restless'. Looking at a person is communicating.

This boy, Alan, eighteen, quiet, came in club and amongst the hustle and bustle, the noise of the juke box, screams and shouts – he sat alone. Most people know at least one other person in a club like ours. Alan did, but he sat alone. He sat alone night after night. Geoff, our senior team leader at the time, often referred to Alan in our de-brief meetings after club. He pressed us to the task. 'Has anyone made contact with Alan?' Some workers had tried. 'Yes' or 'No' answers were his only responses to their gentle questions and comments. He sat leaning forward, elbows and forearms on thighs, head slightly bowed, watching the pool game every night.

Each side of the pool table there are seats, one side comfortable, moulded plastic ones that create interaction with room to seat four or more in a friendly squash. The other side, which Alan frequented, was a bench, not so comfortable. This is an obvious piece of body language. Alan sat alone, with little interaction or response to peers or workers. His posture declared his unhappiness and we all read it.

Then one night he came in to club, put his 10p on the table to reserve the next game, and moved his seating position to the other side of the table! That evening in the de-brief meeting we all rejoiced! People may think we are nuts – but Alan had become secure enough to move his body to another seat and it was, to us, a sign of growth. Some Christians may say that this is a long way from seeing a teenager become a Christian, and they are right. Yet our work in Jesus' name is starting *where people are at* and nurturing their development into the wholeness that Jesus came and died for. In Alan we looked for the smallest signs of growth, and that's what we have to do, and we saw it. That night Geoff led us in a prayer of thankfulness.

In youth work it is so important to develop the skill of reading 'body language'. Some youth and community work courses commence their whole period of professional training with a module of observation exercises. Jesus said we have eyes to see, but we do not see. It seems to me as a Christian and a youth worker, that it is very important to be able to read and understand body language as well as to learn to control our own.

'Pacing' is a method now used in management training throughout the world. It refers to the skill of reflecting the body posture of someone, to help to establish good relationships. In service industries, or dealing with conflict, or counselling, it is a taught method mainly limited to body language. It is one thing, of course, to pace a client with a view to making a sale, or as an executive going for an interview, to pace the interviewer. In youth work it's different!

We can also pace people verbally. Our speed, tone, pitch can be paced so as to help the empathy process. I often do this body language pacing without even thinking – it has become subconscious. Sitting alongside Alan, leaning forward watching the pool game, I would unthinkingly reflect a very similar posture. I wouldn't, for instance, pull up a chair in front of him and stare into his eyes! I don't think many people would.

As a Christian, because that is what I am before anything

else, I study 'the man': the person of Jesus who was perfect and, because he is alive today, remains perfect. In the Bible we read of his awareness of body language and, indeed, his sensitive use of his own body.

'Jesus noticed some of the guests were choosing the best places . . . (Luke 14:7). Yes, Jesus noticed or read the scene on numerous occasions. On this occasion He communicated by using a short story – a parable – concrete communication.

'A woman . . . she was bent over and could not straighten up . . . when Jesus saw her.' (Luke 13:11). Jesus saw, read and understood. He observed an individual so He could read that person's need to the very depth. Jesus' encounter with the woman caught in adultery (John 8:2-11) gives some fascinating examples of his use of body language: '. . . he sat down and began to teach them.' '. . . brought in a woman who had been caught committing adultery and made her stand before them all.' '. . . he bent over and wrote on the ground with his finger.' '. . . he straightened up and said to them . . .' 'then he bent over again . . .' 'He straightened himself up and said to her . . .' These may all seem very insignificant body movements but I am sure they are quite significant in how Jesus was relating to the teachers of the law and this woman who was under accusation. The difference between talking face to face and talking from a different level (e.g. near the ground) has quite an effect on the person you are talking to.

Jesus' use of touch also is very significant – in healing and otherwise, 'he touched the man's ear and healed him.' (Luke 22:51). There are many examples of this.

Jesus has a whole repertoire of skills – the whole package. To be growing as a Christian means extending our repertoire and that, in this case, means knowing how to read the language of the body.

The boys were outside kicking the club door again. They

were on a suspension from club. Only a week before they had reached a peak of violence. They had been smashing numerous car windows and stealing from them. They then steamed the club swinging iron bars and broken cues. Then six of them had acquired a scaffold pole and rammed it with force at my office window. All our windows are made of unbreakable glass (it was either board them up and live in darkness, or grill them up and create an environment of hostility and defence – or this type of glass). It wasn't therefore the window that broke but the frame smashed and splintered as the glass bent to allow the metal pole through. I was upset because 'Gloria' my canary caught the full whack on its cage/home. That's the nearest Gloria has got to flying for some time. Yes, she is OK thanks!

Now the boys were back, eight of them. I went out to face the hostility while the door was locked behind me. They were only sixteen/seventeen years of age but I faced a barrage of all sorts of abuse and questioning. Legs apart, arms by their sides, fists clenching and unclenching, jaws tight and teeth prominent, the leaders of the group were frustrated and angry. I could have stayed with my back to the closed club door and facing them stood my ground. That is what I felt like doing. It was much harder to wander across the pavement towards them, thirty feet away. I felt I had to, though. Still chatting in a warm but firm way, I bent down, feet in the gutter and bum on the kerb. The boys had moved with me, still slagging me off. Circling me and kicking stones around with aggression. I picked up the pebbles from the gutter and flicked them across the road with my thumb. I felt my back vulnerable as they moved around me like restless wolves.

Before long, however, I was joined in the gutter by one, and then two, until most sat in a line talking while the others crouched in the road, facing me, only moving for cars going past. We chatted on – and the words became friendlier and the conversation more positive – that leads into another story, but . . .

The analysis of this was – I had deliberately taken a non-aggressive body posture. I had made myself vulnerable, very hard to do under such circumstances (my trained mind told me to do it, my emotions were telling me to run in and slam the door or at least keep my back protected). The boys had 'paced' me and had followed me into a non-aggressive posture. They had a limited repertoire in dealing with conflict – 'Fight or flight' – i.e. fight your way out of aggro – or, if well down the pecking order – damn well run!

I have a larger repertoire and was able to think alongside my strange emotions and decide on how best to steer the situation, morally, verbally, and non-verbally.

Reading and understanding body language isn't just an interesting subject – in a hostile environment it can be dangerous not to. It is an important part of letting Jesus live through us. Not doing it can also be insensitive, non-developmental and not of the Kingdom. So often Christian students all huddle together, laughing and chatting in the college canteen and do not even see the isolated student sitting alone at the next table. That is *non-shalom*. 'Blessed are the Shalom-makers'.

Chapter 8

References

1. David Sheppard, Dimbleby Lecture 1984 and *The Listener* April 1984.
2. David Sheppard, *Built as a City* (Hodder and Stoughton 1974).
3. Jim Punton
4. T. A. Harris, *I'm OK – You're OK*.
5. John Adair, *Effective Leadership* (Pan 1983).
6. David Sheppard, *Bias to the Poor*.
7. M. Herbert, *Problems of Childhood* (Pan 1975).
8. Jane Gabraith.
9. Max Warren, *Crowded Canvas* (Hodder and Stoughton 1974).
10. Bennie E. Goodwin II, *The Effective Leader: A Basic Guide to Christian Leadership* (IVP Illinois 1971).

9: A real gospel for real people

When we first came to the Mayflower, I remember walking through the dingy club corridors and thinking to myself, 'It is going to be a big job here.' Five years had seemed a long stretch at the 'Y' Club. This place, I thought, needs a ten year commitment.

One year later I was praying this over. After *one* year it was really too hard to continue. Too painful! We prayed and evaluated so much, especially when things were extremely violent and emotionally stressful, and again and again over the years I asked myself, 'How can anyone do this job?' In fact it was ten years later that it was right to move. All connections came together through real prayer and a now grown family making the decision in a real participation exercise. Little did I know when this book was commissioned, two years before, that its completion would coincide with the Mayflower journey coming to an end for my family.

With Joy, eighteen and Ann, twelve, and Joan and I having celebrated our twentieth wedding anniversary, we have now moved home and commitment to Romford YMCA. A new life has opened before us, having learned so much from Canning Town people and from a team of youth workers that shine with love, humour, commitment and the fruits of the Spirit.

What can I say to end this 'book journey' of reflection which I've shared with you. I've tried to be honest, open and balanced. My main purpose has been to tell you how it is on the streets and in the clubs where 'underside' young people gather. I wanted you to feel their gutter feelings. I wanted you to feel their pain. Also my own hurts and those of family and colleagues. Some of them have come out. All this places me, them and us in a vulnerable position. If you were interacting with me, instead of only reading, I wouldn't feel vulnerable because we would be in real communication, *two-way* communication, face to face. One-way communication is inadequate, and this is another reason why we as youth workers feel vulnerable – we *need* feed-back.

That is exactly why Jesus was God's Word, in *flesh*. The whole message of the incarnation is to establish true, two-way communication. That is why I have shared with you my faith and the experiences shared with others with whom I work.

I've not got a big enough mind to know all the answers to deprivation, numbness, juvenile crime. However, I do know it's a lot to do with God, because He cares, He showed it in Jesus and He still shows it. A lot also is to do with social organisation; how we organise ourselves as a society can damage, build up, destroy or develop. A society can love like an individual does if it gets itself organised. Band-Aid proved it recently with their raising of over half a billion pounds for the Ethiopia famine. Archbishop Temple has been quoted as saying that, 'the primary form of love in social organisation is Justice'. We live in an unjust society and most of us sit back in our armchairs and accept it!

I sometimes feel really bad about our family not owning our own home. It makes me insecure to know that for the past twenty years our home has come with my job and one day we will be without one. Most of my peers in the north-west have almost complete mortgages and nice homes. So have so many 'just married' couples and nearly every Christian I know. When I do think about it I feel really bad about it and yet I have no right to! Canning Town families live in council property (and very few in *houses*), so why should I deserve my own three-bedroomed semi with a garden? And compare even the poorest Canning Town family with most families in Ethiopia!

I do know that the answer to these problems is a lot to do with God, social organisation, the individual and the Church. Being assured and guaranteed our heavenly place, joy and *shalom* that passes all understanding, we have a biblical commission, from start to finish, to establish His Kingdom *on earth*. The Church, both the individuals and the organisation, needs to be an example of love, justice and joy. I sometimes feel bad about the 'house thing' (as described above) because of what I see as 'normal'. We, as Christians need to be setting new norms.

How do people see Christians? 'I don't read the Bible – I read you' said a club kid! How do they see the Church?

Stan and Eddie dropped in one day. I had last seen Stan when he came out of prison; our relationship has developed via many letters. I don't think I'd seen Eddie for about five years. They are both twenty-seven years old now. So we sat on the juke-box, drinking coffee and just reflecting. But then, in the midst of talking about how drug use was now an accepted part of life in the East End, Eddie said, 'We've done everything now – booze, thieving, drugs, girls – there's nothing else to do.' 'What about God?' I asked, 'or does God not fit the East End image?'

This provoked a conversation about the Government and the 'Old Bill': 'There's a lot of poverty around here now, Pip. Once the pubs were crowded – now they're half empty and even our mates ponce (beg) drinks all night . . . there's going to be riots . . . people are going to join with the blacks and there'll be riots.'

What they were saying was fascinating in itself, but what struck me with such force was that they were talking about God in the same breath as the Government and the police. So, with controlled enthusiasm, I talked with them of the 'underside Jesus' who, when physically on earth, spent his time with the leper, the prostitute, the thief, the stigmatised. He did not act as one in authority and with status.

Stan and Eddie were writing off God as they do a distant oppressive authority! We have got to come down, as groups of people, and not stay 'topside' in positions of safety, comfort and status. 'Get lost' theology is risky, a 'Get out' theology isn't for me, you could say. The Church Missionary Society used the following on their adverts: 'Has God called you to stay where you are?' Unless someone moves Ethiopia stays as it is and the inner city stays as it is. I am aware that there is more to this argument, but you can see the point: 'If you're not part of the solution you're part of the problem.'

Some inner-city Christians say 'keep out – you do more damage than good!' That is true – unless the 'underside' way is taken and people come in to learn, not to give. Roger Sainsbury presented a paper at Greenbelt Festival in 1983, describing the cultural attitudes and norms that need to be abandoned by the middle-class people coming into the inner city. The differences he outlined were:

Middle Class	Working Class
Individuality	Group loyalty
Judgmental	Accepting/kind
Privacy	Openness
Stiff upper lip	Vulnerability
Facts	Feelings
Meetings	Meeting[1]

Joy Sansom, Mayflower voluntary team member, speaks of herself and others coming as middle class, 'from outside the area . . . from a culture that is "dominant" . . . from those sections of society which have power and control'. When starting a Christian discipleship group Joy admits that it was Joyce, a local Christian woman with her own children and grandchildren, 'that caused the group to happen. The fact she was local and respected . . . without her it would have disintegrated. *She* was the girls' point of reference. I represented Christianity to them, who they didn't really know, understand or even like . . .'

I believe that Jesus spent thirty years learning from the people He was to minister to. Like a sponge He soaked in the culture – everything that was meaningful. As a child He 'grew and developed in body, mind and spirit', the Bible says, 'in favour with both God and man' (Luke 1:80; 2:52 Living Bible).

'Our social background affects the way we understand the Christian gospel and the Scriptures,' Roger Sainsbury said. 'It's not a different gospel but seen from a different vantage point.' He gives another list of differences:

Middle Class	Working Class
Formulas	Drama
Theory	Action (Praxis)
Status (Right with God)	Active Goodness
Personal Righteousness	Social Justice
Omnipotent Lord	Human Jesus[2]

Tony Campolo, an American speaker, popular in this country, agrees. 'If you read the Bible with a set of middle-class values, guess what you'll find in the Bible? Middle-class values . . .'[3] Another illustration comes from Joy Sansom again.

Only having recently moved into the area (1982) my only experience of sharing the gospel at that time was in direct verbal and Bible-orientated ways, and so we started having Bible studies.

This didn't last very long as the girls couldn't relate to the method or to me. It was a totally inappropriate way of sharing the gospel. Firstly, because the girls were not used to thinking on that level or reading from the Bible and discussing, and secondly because they could not relate it to their own lives, it seemed totally irrelevant – and probably was.

Gradually, amidst much despondency, I realised this and we started taking the emphasis off straight Bible study and instead began sharing more through 'relevant' discussion, games and just chatting, whenever we could, bringing God-issues in and applying them in simple ways. Gradually the trust and relationships and understanding were built up.

This discipling and sharing of faith came from activity that was not based on a printed page – much like the disciples of Jesus who didn't carry a New Testament in their back pockets!

I have often referred to the difference between thinking I 'concepts' and in 'concrete' terms. It seems to me that middle-class people, generally, think in concepts while working-class people think in a concrete way. For instance a concrete mind will transfer a communication onto a little mental video screen and play it like a picture show. Concepts can't be projected – concrete communication can.

That's why I love that passage in Matthew 13:13, when Jesus' disciples came to Him and asked why He used parables. Jesus replied: '. . . the reason I use parables in talking to them is that they look but do not see, and they listen, but do not hear or understand . . .' Stories can be played onto the video screen, and yet 99% of all Christian literature is conceptional and doesn't relate to *Sun*, *Daily Mirror* or *Daily Star* readers. Jim Punton, F.Y.T. training officer, is quoted as saying, 'the word became flesh, but most of us Christians would be more comfortable if the *flesh* became *word*.'

Morris Stuart reminds us that, 'Most of the world's Christians are either illiterate or semi-literate. The startling fact is that it is in these places, where illiterate Christians live and work, that God seems to be most at work. Literacy for all God's people does not seem to be essential for their spiritual growth and power.'[4] You are no less a Christian if you can't read or articulate in 'spiritual' jargon. The communication needs to be relevant to the human culture that we are in.

The gospel must relate to the context we are in. In a middle-class environment this can, acceptably, be more intellectual, more personal, but in a different environment where injustice, oppression, and poverty abound – the gospel *must* speak to all of this as well – we can't just say 'Turn to Jesus and everything will be fine.'

This leads on to the whole issue of Conversion, which is one area I have shared about personally, as regards my own experience, and generally as far as the inner city goes. To make it clear – I *am* for it! But having expressed a clear commitment to conversion, biblically and experientially, I have other conclusions also. Many of my own friends and younger brothers and sisters have 'been converted' to a living faith in Jesus – and remain in it. Others I know not remained. Whole groups of Mayflower kids a Christian commitment and are now One member who became a Chris sentence and who, as a community, we have spent hours with, has been given two life sentences for the murder of a woman and her pre-school age child. Others have since followed a life of serious crime and made personal and emotional disasters of their lives. More importantly they have hardened their hearts against a God who in *their* terms 'doesn't work'.

From my experience this is clearly linked with deprivation of the inner-city kind. 'Go and make disciples', has not been my experience amongst the 'hard' kids – not permanent disciples anyway – while with the more stable, secure people in inner city, or elsewhere, I have known far more long-term life-changing experiences. That is my experience. There are exceptions, of course, but people often don't realise how few these exceptions are. Because they are so unusual they are brought to people's attention, by giving testimonies – or writing a book!

I believe now that we must be very sensitive to our evangelistic task and not press for 'conversion experiences' which end up actually turning people away from Jesus who loves and died for them. We need to love these kids so much that their complete wholeness comes before a quick 'conversion experience'. That may mean a slow informal encour the young person to encourage con on-making ability. Trusting and ortant decision – the eternal one –

few words about education
worked as an unqualified
old I became a profes-
urse for youth and
good points about
n removed from

society to become a 'student' or be pressed into the mould of 'academia'! My placements during the three were largely at Mayflower so the theory always applied to real long-term practice, not short-term placement.

I am pleased to see ministers in the Anglican Church now being trained via the 'non-stipendiary courses' for the same reasons. It's a pity, however, that so much training is still academic and facilitated by 100% middle-class staff. Jim Gosling, a 'non-stipendiary' and an ex-Mayflower club member and Sunday Group boy, now a probation officer, stood preaching in the Mayflower Chapel when a stone was lobbed through the stained glass window and showered him with glass. 'There was nothing on my course about this sort of thing,' he said.

Jim has been critical of his training and would agree with the Newham Deanery Submission to the Archbishop's Commission for Urban Priority Areas, which says that, 'Too often (the typical clergy) are products of middle-class areas and their experience of college training is totally unrelated to preparing them for inner-urban ministry.'

Even with more relevant training, the minister or youth worker cannot work in isolation. I believe that the toughest inner-city situation needs a team work approach: interdependency among a team who can support each other by sharing experiences and biblical insight. I really do believe that each team needs a theological input. If, for instance, the youth worker or Family Care worker is under pressure for a time, the whole team needs to emotionally support that worker and apply that experience theologically. There is so much to learn from God *in* each other. Experience is so important because each community is so different, and it is necessary for the gospel to be 'contextualised'.

We must present a real gospel for the real people – of the

community. To have an evangelist coming into a community without totally *listening* and *integrating* into an inner-city team, can, in my experience (not just my opinion), totally unsettle a long-term work for God.

Ideally, the staff turnover of a large team ministry centre or group of churches will be so slow that each new member can build on the work and experience with his or her freshness, without setting it back.

Speaking as a youth worker on the frontier, we need a team to relate with and not work in isolation. This way we will be able to work out the gospel in context *together*. Too many youth workers and church ministers work in isolation and this can only be bad news in the inner city.

I walked up to Canning Town's Rathbone Market today. It was lunch-time, and not many young people about yet, but lots of elderly beautiful people to chat to. Old Arthur, a widower, came up and 'borrowed' enough for a cup of tea. This is very unusual; most East Enders have a pride that makes them survive—and more. It was a privilege to give, though. The giving has often been the other way—they are the most generous community I've known. There is so much character, gentleness, generosity and warmth around. The real Cockney atmosphere is evident from the cheerful stall-holders, Mayflower members and hundreds of other contacts. Some would see just poor people and, if you stay with the basic economic facts they would be correct. But richness goes beyond just money. I've been enriched by the poor *and* the rich many times over.

> 'Seek the Shalom of the City where I have sent you . . . and pray to the Lord on its behalf; for in its Shalom you will find your own Shalom.'
> (Jeremiah 29:6-7)

Chapter 9

References

1. Roger Sainsbury, *An Amber Light*.
2. Roger Sainsbury, (op. cit.).
3. Tony Campolo, *Buzz magazine* (April 1984).
4. Morris Stuart, *On Being* (published in Australia).

If you wish to receive *regular information* about *new books,* please send your name and address to:

London Bible Warehouse
PO Box 123
Basingstoke
Hants RG23 7NL

Name _____

Address _____

_____

_____

_____

I am especially interested in:
- [ ] Biographies
- [ ] Fiction
- [ ] Christian living
- [ ] Issue related books
- [ ] Academic books
- [ ] Bible study aids
- [ ] Children's books
- [ ] Music
- [ ] Other subjects

P.S. If you have ideas for new Christian Books or other products, please write to us too!

THROUGH DAVID'S PSALMS

Derek Prince

Derek Prince, internationally known Bible teacher and scholar, draws on his understanding of the Hebrew language and culture, and a comprehensive knowledge of Scripture, to present 101 meditations from the Psalms.

Each of these practical and enriching meditations is based on a specific passage and concludes with a faith response. They can be used either for personal meditation or for family devotions. They are intended for all those who want their lives enriched or who seek comfort and encouragement from the Scriptures.

LOVING GOD

Charles Colson

Loving God is the very purpose of the believer's life, the vocation for which he is made. However loving God is not easy and most people have given little real thought to what the greatest commandment really means.

Many books have been written on the individual subjects of repentence, Bible study, prayer, outreach, evangelism, holiness and other elements of the Christian life. In **Loving God**, Charles Colson draws all these elements together to look at the entire process of growing up as a Christian.

Combining vivid illustrations with straightforward exposition he shows how to live out the Christian faith in our daily lives. **Loving God** provides a real challenge to deeper commitment and points the way towards greater maturity.